THROWING BULLETS

ALSO BY ROY ROWAN

The Four Days of Mayaguez (1975)

The Intuitive Manager (1986)

A Day in the Life of Italy (1989) Coeditor

Powerful People (1996)

First Dogs (1997)

Surfcaster's Quest (1999)

Solomon Starbucks Striper (2003)

Chasing the Dragon (2004)

THROWING BULLETS

A TALE OF TWO PITCHERS CHASING THE DREAM

ROY ROWAN

TAYLOR TRADE PUBLISHING
Lanham • New York • Boulder • Toronto • Oxford

Published by Taylor Trade Publishing
An imprint of The Rowman & Littlefield Publishing Group, Inc.
4501 Forbes Boulevard, Suite 200, Lanham, Maryland 20706

Distributed by NATIONAL BOOK NETWORK

Library of Congress Cataloging-in-Publication Data

Rowan, Roy.
Throwing bullets : a tale of two pitchers chasing the dream / Roy Rowan.
p.   cm.
Includes index.
ISBN-13: 978-1-58979-367-5 (cloth : alk. paper)
ISBN-10: 1-58979-367-6 (cloth : alk. paper)
1. Pitchers (Baseball)—Biography.   2. Olson, Justin.
3. Liriano, Francisco.   I. Title.
GV865.A1R69   2006
796.357092'2—dc22
2006002626

∞ ™ The paper used in this publication meets the minimum requirements
of American National Standard for Information Sciences—Permanence of
Paper for Printed Library Materials, ANSI/NISO Z39.48-1992.

Manufactured in the United States of America.

For Helen

Rain or shine,
She sat through them all.

CONTENTS

CONTENTS

1

JUSTIN VERSUS FRANCISCO

It is Friday evening, the start of the Memorial Day weekend, and the New Britain Rock Cats are playing host to the New Hampshire Fisher Cats in the first of a four-game series. The disappearing sun is still drenching the lush green field punctuated with white bases in late afternoon light. Both teams have taken their licks in the batting cage and the 7,500 seats are beginning to fill with fans already munching hot dogs, spareribs, super-pretzels, and popcorn.

Out in front of the modern red brick and steel stadium, Bill Dowling, former vice president and general counsel of the New York Yankees, and now president, general manager, and part owner of the Rock Cats, stands impeccably dressed in a blue blazer, striped tie, and tan slacks, surveying the cars streaming into the blacktopped parking lot.

"Looks like another full house," he predicts optimistically to one of his assistants. Then as if he were the host of a private party being given at his home, he continues greeting many of the arriving ticket-holders with a jovial handshake or friendly slap on the back. "It's like being a congressman," he claims. "These are my constituents and I've got to listen to what they have to say, and let them know that I appreciate the fact they show up to support us."

His team's last-place standing in the Eastern League doesn't seem to have cooled the ardor of the fans from New Britain and Hartford's other suburbs. Fortunately for the Rock Cats, both the Yankee Stadium in the Bronx and Fenway Park in Back Bay, Boston, are for all practical purposes too far to drive, especially for a night game. As a result, the Rock Cats' attendance has grown every year under Dowling's management, which began six years ago, topping 311,000 in 2004. "If the folks around here want to see a baseball game," he says, "this is where they come."

Pleased with prospects of a sellout crowd, Bill heads back inside the stadium, where he roams the cavernous concourse under the stands checking on everything from ticket sales to the cleanliness of the concessions. The food business is leased out to a catering company called Centerplate. But it still produces a healthy chunk of revenue for the New Britain Baseball Club and helps to keep the tickets moderately priced from $3.50 to $10—except for the dozen sky boxes rented for $15,000 a season.

The running of the Rock Cats, I discovered, is a business

of brothers. Bill and his sibling Bob Dowling, director of media relations, take care of the administrative side, while the Cliburn twins, Stan the field manager, and Stew the pitching coach, handle the young players, all of whom are the property of the Minnesota Twins and in effect merely on loan for the summer to their Double-A farm team, the Rock Cats.

As the sky darkens, the thick grove of willows, pines, and maples growing up to the outfield fence casts cool shadows on the field. Suddenly the lights snap on and Francisco Liriano, the Rock Cats' ace left-hander from the Dominican Republic, begins throwing his warm-up pitches. Each time his wiry, 6-foot-2 frame unwinds, the ball flies from his fingers, appearing as little more than a white streak as it shoots across home plate. It pops the leather of the catcher's mitt so hard it sounds like a gunshot, even to the fans sitting high up at the Sam Adams Terrace bar and grill atop the left-field grandstand. Barbequed ribs, Italian sausages, and chicken breasts, sizzling over a charcoal fire up there, waft waves of mouthwatering aromas over the entire stadium.

For a few minutes all eyes in the stadium are fastened on the illuminated pitch-speed gauge mounted on the right-field fence as it flashes 94, 95, 96, then—wow!—97 miles per hour. Liriano may be the fastest pitcher in the minors. He has been compared to his Venezuelan idol, Johan Santana, who won the American League 2004 Cy Young Award pitching for the Twins, the big-league club Liriano hopes to be throwing bullets for some day in the future. New Britain fans are quick to embrace their young heroes, and he is one of the reasons for the large Friday night turnout.

A color guard of flag bearers marches smartly out behind the mound. They are followed by a wisp of a grammar school girl, barely 4 feet tall, singing the "Star-Spangled Banner." When she falters halfway through it, having memorized "America the Beautiful" by mistake, the sympathetic crowd comes to her rescue. In unison they chorus all of the missing words before giving her a huge ovation as she disappears into the home team's dugout.

Ominous clouds blot out the sun as the plate umpire cries: "Play ball!" Liriano uncorks a 96-mph fastball for strike one. He gets safely through the first inning, giving up just one base on balls. In the second inning he strikes out the first batter, but the next hitter singles, quickly steals second, goes to third on a long fly ball, and then scores on another base hit. Liriano looks like he's in trouble. But after the third single of the inning, he overpowers the next Fisher Cats' batter with three successive fastballs and trots back to the dugout.

By the beginning of the third, with the Rock Cats trailing 1 to 0, the clouds form a black canopy blanketing the ballpark. Jagged lightning streaks dance crazily across the sky, outshining the brightly lit scoreboard in center field bearing the scowling, furry face of what presumably is a rock cat.

"Looks like we don't need any fireworks tonight," blares the voice of the game announcer over the public address system. Fireworks were a popular postgame attraction on Friday nights until a group of neighbors filed a suit claiming the fiery bombardments kept them awake, forcing the Rock Cats to limit the displays to once a month. The announcer also reminds the crowd that it's "Sleep Well Night," a promotion for Gaylord Hospital's Department of Sleep Disorders. Prizes, he explains, will be awarded to fans displaying the most colorful pajamas after those innings in which the Rock Cats' pitcher puts the opposing batters to sleep.

A few raindrops peck at the carefully groomed infield dirt and mound where Liriano appears to be gaining strength and rhythm after his shaky start. Working rapidly as if trying to beat the gathering storm as well as the Fisher Cats, he gets a called strike on the first batter, then is distracted as skies start to open up, loses his concentration and fires two balls way out of the strike zone.

Torrents of rain whip across the field, sending the players racing to their dugouts and most of the fans scurrying for cover in the concourse under the grandstand. Viewed from the press box, the floodlights look like they are being sprayed by fire hoses as the soaked groundskeeping crew, assisted by a dozen or so hardy volunteers from the bleachers, heave and haul to unroll the cumbersome plastic tarp until it finally covers the infield. The tarp quickly fills with water prompting a couple of show-offs in the crowd to peel off their shoes and socks, race out onto the field, and, with a running start, bodysurf across the inundated plastic, skidding 40 or 50 feet on their bellies before coming to a stop. The diehards still huddled under the covered section of the grandstand emit a feeble cheer. Meanwhile, back in the clubhouse with his teammates, Liriano wraps his arm in hot towels, trying to keep it warm and loose enough to fire more of his 95-, 96-, and 97-mile-an-hour bullets if the deluge ends and play is resumed.

The rain finally does slow to a drizzle and the tarp is rolled back up, leaving two large lakes behind short and second. Now armed with push brooms, the groundskeepers try desperately to disperse the water, but to no avail. The lakes keep re-forming behind their brooms, forcing the sweepers to go back and start all over again.

Every 30 minutes or so the three umpires, resembling a trio of funeral directors in their black suits, emerge from the Fisher Cats' dugout and march in lockstep across the field to inspect its condition. They squish through the wet grass on their way to examine the two lakes. General Manager Dowling, highly visible in a yellow slicker and obviously loathe to lose the ticket receipts of a near-sellout crowd, marches right along with the umpires, hoping to convince them that if they'll just be patient and allow the drainage system to do its job the drenched field will be playable. Then they all march back together and disappear into the dugout again without informing the few remaining fans of their decision. Finally, after a rain-delay of precisely 2 hours and 21 minutes (the time was announced over the PA system) and several more round-trips out onto the field by Bill and the umpires, good sense prevails and the game is suspended, to be continued the next afternoon as the first part of a Saturday doubleheader.

That is a bad break for Liriano, who has given up three hits, a walk, and a run, and only struck out two, not one of his best performances. He counted on improving as the game progressed. But the 45 pitches he had thrown, many of them bullets in two-and-one-third innings, were enough to earn him several days' rest. So if the Rock Cats went down to defeat the next day without ever tying the Fisher Cats, he would be charged with the defeat—his fifth against one victory.

Saturday afternoon sparkled with sunlight as the two teams took the field to resume play. Right-hander Justin Olson, a former Big Ten star, was called on to pick up where Liriano left off—an ironic situation since the two pitchers were friends and had come up to New Britain from the Single-A Fort Myers Miracle together, sharing the same mound and the same dream of a big-league career. But in a way they were competing to see who could throw the most strikeouts, achieve the lowest earned run average, and win the most games, and thereby get a shot at the "show," their word for the majors.

The two pitchers couldn't have been more different. Liriano, a 21-year-old lefty and the son of a poor Dominican cowherd, was plucked off the sandlots of Santo Domingo and signed as a free agent center fielder in 2000 by the San Francisco Giants. Impressed by the way the 16-year-old could fire a ball whistling on a straight line from deep in the outfield to home plate, the Giants soon converted him into a pitcher, but then threw him in as part of a trade for the Twins' hard-hitting catcher, A.J. Pierzynski.

Olson, a 25-year-old right-hander, and the product of a solid, middle-class American family, was not only a standout athlete at the University of Illinois, but an all–Big Ten academic star, graduating with a teaching degree in kinesiology. He, too, was signed as a nondrafted free agent while pitching for the Rockford, Illinois, River Hawks in the independent Frontier League. Both men had demonstrated poise, strength, and an overpowering fastball. And they were both big, something the scouts viewed with favor. Liriano, standing 6-feet-2, weighs 185 pounds, while Olson, 6-3, weighs 215.

The two men, however, employ strikingly different pitching styles. Olson stands on the mound absolutely still between pitches, all business and concentration. He is more laid-back, less fast and less flashy, but often more efficient than Liriano. Although he can throw 94-mile-an-hour bullets, he works on the premise that it usually takes five or six pitches to strike a man out, but only two or three to get him to pop up or ground out.

Liriano is more high-strung, but usually able to conceal his Latin temperament on the mound. With his long, lean legs, his loose hips, and ropelike throwing motion, he works fast—sometimes too fast—striving, it seems, to strike out every batter, but running up high counts, which possibly explain the elbow injury that kept him on the sidelines most of the 2002 and 2003 seasons. But he's back on full power this year. In the 43 games preceding the rained-out game against the Fisher Cats, he struck out 69 batters in 57 innings.

Despite their differences, the two pitchers show great promise. "They're both good listeners and eager to learn," claims Rock Cats' pitching coach Stew Cliburn, who has helped a number of young hurlers prepare themselves for the majors by improving what he and other pitching coaches call their "mechanics"—a term suggesting to me that they regard a pitching arm as some kind of machine that, with slight adjustments, can be made to operate more efficiently. But even with his improved mechanics, Olson knows he probably never will be able to match Liriano's blazing speed, which is why the Dominican was already on Minnesota's 40-man roster, giving him the chance that Olson didn't really have, of being called up by the Twins come this September.

Called on to finish the game that Liriano started the previous night, Olson was cruising along smoothly in his unspectacular workmanlike fashion, striking out a couple of batters, giving up a run, but keeping the Rock Cats in range of the Fisher Cats until the fifth inning when Rob Crosby came to bat. Hardly considered a slugger, Crosby had hit only one home run since the start of the season.

Olson seemed to have his number, tossing two quick strikes. But on his next pitch, the sharp crack of wood connecting with cowhide could have been heard all the way over on Route 9 several blocks away. Center fielder Jim Tomlin, whose grandfather played with Satchel Page on the Kansas City Monarchs, turned his head, but never bothered to take a step backward as the white ball, still gaining altitude, soared 20 feet above the 400-foot mark on the green fence and disappeared among the willow trees in back of the stadium. Home run balls were Olson's nemesis. After the game when I mentioned to him how sorry I was to see that ball sail over the center field fence, he answered tersely, but with a smile, "You and me both!"

"That pitch was supposed to be a slider," explained pitching coach Stew Cliburn. "But it was spinning sideways instead of down when Crosby connected. Olson didn't get his fingers on top of the ball as he was supposed to—simply a mechanical failure."

Maybe it was Olson's lack of concentration that afternoon. He had recently received the unsettling news that he'd lost his starting spot on the five-man rotation, and was being relegated to the bull pen. During the 2004 season in Fort Myers, he had done yeoman service as a relief pitcher as well as a starter and felt comfortable in both roles. Being assigned to the pen wouldn't necessarily kill his chances of moving up the Twins' hierarchy. Reliable closers are always in short supply. Still, starters are the stars and usually attract more attention.

The demotion, if you could call it that, wasn't really Olson's fault. His three-and-three win-loss record was better than Liriano's, and pretty good considering that the Rock Cats were then bogged down in the Eastern League basement. While Liriano had been pitching well, averaging better than one strikeout per inning, the Rock Cats' batters seemed to fall into a stupor every time he took the mound. They just couldn't get him any runs. "They stand like statues at the plate, waiting for a pitch more to their liking," the exasperated manager, Stan Cliburn complained. "One of the first things we do with these young hitters is teach them where the strike zone is, and tell them to take a cut at the ball when it's there."

His coaching, however, apparently had fallen on deaf ears or dead bats. As a result the team had been shut out 10 times in its first 44 games, compared to 9 times during the entire 2004 season. Even worse, the Rock Cats' batters seemed unable to foul off enough good pitches to draw an occasional base on balls. As of the start of the Memorial Day weekend, the team had gone 22 consecutive innings without one man getting a walk.

Eight days after serving up Rob Crosby's disastrous home run blast, Olson was called on again to relieve Liriano—this time in an away game against the Portland Sea Dogs. The Dominican had just come off the mound after a terrible night. His throwing rhythm was off, his slider had no bite, and his fastball lacked its usual late action. In five innings he had given up six runs on seven hits and two walks before being yanked.

Entering the game with no outs in the eighth, and with the Rock Cats trailing 9 to 8, Olson proceeded to strike out the next three batters while holding the Sea Dogs scoreless. Then to the amazement of the Portland fans familiar with New Britain's puny clutch hitting, the Rock Cats' bats suddenly came alive in the ninth, rattling base hits all around the ballpark to score an impressive 12 to 9 victory, with reliever Justin Olson gaining the win. "Some nights you just get lucky," he said. Then with his usual modesty added, "It was the hitters that did it. Not me."

2

MORE DISNEY
THAN DOUBLEDAY

Justin Olson and Francisco Liriano are participants in what
amounts to a major renaissance in minor-league baseball. It's
a coast-to-coast phenomena produced by teams with such
odd, nonbaseball-sounding names as Quakes (Rancho Cuca-
monga, California), Lugnuts (Lansing, Michigan), Curve
(Altoona, Pennsylvania), and Thunder (Trenton, New Jer-
sey). Yet, these ball clubs are among 226 professional outfits
in towns and suburbs, playing their hearts out in clean, modern stadiums (eight new ones opened in 2005), where many
of the special facilities and services offered are not usually
associated with baseball—picnic pavilions, playgrounds, hot
tubs, rock climbing walls, even wine gardens.

I first got hooked on minor-league baseball while writing an article for *Fortune* magazine in 2000 on the business reasons for its fast-growing popularity. A photographer and I flew all around the country attending games in different leagues and in different surroundings, from the California desert to the Maine seacoast. By the time we completed the circuit, I'd become an ardent fan, though many new attractions and amenities have since been added.

A hot dog cannon at the Sacramento River Cats' stadium now fires free foil-wrapped franks into the crowd. The Dayton Dragons promise free back rubs on Friday and Saturday nights, possibly to relieve the tension of a close game, or more likely a bad week at the office. Both the Reading Phillies and Corpus Christi Hooks (owned by Hall of Fame pitcher Nolan Ryan and his two sons) have stadium swimming pools just beyond the right-field fence, so homers literally make a big splash. And speaking of splashes, the Charleston, South Carolina, River Dogs occasionally urge their fans to come dressed in bathing suits for some of their broiling 100-plus-degree day games, because they are likely to get sprayed with fire hoses courtesy of Smuckers' jams.

These crowd-pleasing shenanigans, often promoting some product or company, go on almost every summer day in every minor-league park. And in Pawtucket, Rhode Island, they periodically continue all night. Several times a season the Pawtucket Red Sox, or "PawSox" as they're known, invite a thousand or more boys and girls to bring tents and blankets for a postgame party and sleepover in the outfield. The better the entertainment, it appears, the bigger the crowd.

"I learned that lesson in my first season as general manager of Rock Cats," Bill Dowling explained. "We lost 19 games in a row. It was pitiful. The score would be 7 or 8 to nothing at the end of the first inning. Things were so bad we finished the season 40 games under the 500 mark. Even if we'd had a winning season, I knew we had to offer more than just baseball." So the Rock Cats, like the other minor-league clubs, started scripting between-innings entertainment and promotional giveaways to make the games more fun for the entire family, especially for the women and children.

Accessibility is another key attraction of the minors. Most of the stadiums are easily reachable by car, a few on foot, like Frontier Field in Rochester, and in the case of Bridgeport, also by rail—so close I've seen a home run there ricochet off a passing Metro-North commuter train. Best of all, every one of these modern, newly designed stadiums features field boxes planted virtually on the diamond, so you can almost reach out and touch the young players.

What also makes these costly and beautifully equipped new stadiums ($72 million for the one recently built by the Memphis Redbirds) so pleasing, is the inexpensive, fan-friendly experience they provide. The parking is easy, tickets are cheap (generally $2 to $10), and so are the souvenirs, food, and sodas—at least compared to prices in the money-crazed big leagues. For the Rock Cats' fans who come on Wednesday nights, there's even a special family deal: four grandstand tickets, four hot dogs, four sodas, and four popcorns, all for $29—certainly a better bargain than the movies.

Almost completely absent from minor-league games is

the rowdiness that oftentimes mars an afternoon or evening at the "Bigs." The crowds are much better behaved. Imagine, sodas and beer still being sold in bottles, not in paper cups, as they are in most major-league parks because of the danger of an irate fan beaning an umpire after a disputed call. With so many services, amenities, and the friendly atmosphere, it's not surprising that more than 41 million fans turned out last year to watch what used to be considered bush-league baseball.

Even so baseball is still the main attraction. And today the minor-leaguers often put on a more exciting show than their big-league brothers. Hoping to catch the eye of a scout or the farm system boss, these aspiring youngsters risk bodily injuries to make spectacular plays that multimillion-dollar big-league players won't chance. As a result, strong-armed young hurlers like Olson and Liriano light up the pitch-speed gauge with fastballs well into the 90s while their acrobatic teammates make what appear to be impossible diving catches, unafraid of tearing a ligament; and base runners dare headlong slides that could fracture a shoulder, or worse yet, break a neck. And the young power hitters swing so hard you'd think they're trying to land a ball on the moon. But these young players can also be as erratic as they are exuberant, booting easy grounders, misjudging flies, and lunging at pitches way out of the strike zone.

Fifty of the teams, like the Bridgeport Bluefish, Long Island Ducks, and Rockford River Hawks, which Olson started playing for, belong to independent leagues, comprised mostly of players still harboring dreams of being scouted and signed for a big-buck bonus, and also aging veterans, many of them big-name cast-offs from the majors. But the other 176 teams are big-league affiliates like the Rock Cats, with coaches and players all being paid and provided by the parent organization.

"That can be both a blessing and a problem," explains Bill Dowling, who winces when one or two of his key players are promoted to the Triple-A Rochester Red Wings before the season is half over. "You have to accept what you get or give up," he says. In the 2000 season his team won the Eastern League championship, mostly with players now starring for the Twins. But in 2005 he was already complaining to anyone in the Minnesota front office who would listen, that his team desperately needed a few power hitters if it was going to climb out of the Eastern League basement. But then the Twins management is more concerned with developing player skills than with the league standing of its farm clubs. "Winning is just the frosting on the cake," claims manager Stan Cliburn, who though a loyal operative in the Twins' farm system, still aspires as his players do to move up to Triple-A Rochester in 2006. (He did.)

Like New Britain, which happens to be exactly 111 miles from both Yankee Stadium and Fenway Park, most of the minor-league franchises are located a safe distance from a major-league city so as not to be competitive. But their popularity has grown so fast that new teams are now also sprouting in big-league backyards. The Brooklyn Cyclones, a Mets' farm in the Single-A, New York-Pennsylvania League, is just a subway ride from Shea Stadium, while the Staten Island Yankees, another new club in that same league, is a subway and ferry ride away from where the Bronx Bombers

17

play. Both of these new teams boast of sellout crowds at all home games.

This bush-league prosperity is a new thing and in a way surprising. In fact, the minors were on the brink of striking out in the early 1970s when total attendance slumped to 10 million. The only thing that kept them alive was the need by the big-league clubs for a pipeline of young talent. And even the talent appeared to be drying up because the dream of playing in the Bigs had faded along with the dwindling number of farm teams to play for.

Lots of things, I found while researching my article for *Fortune*, are behind the resurgence. Movies like *The Natural* (1984) and *Bull Durham* (1988) stimulated interest in the minors, whereas the baseball strike in 1995 had the opposite effect on the majors, embittering many fans that considered the wealthy big-league players a bunch of spoilsports. The major leagues also helped out their farm hands in 1990 by adopting the Facilities Standards Rule, which spells out what minor-league stadiums should look like, from the size of the playing field to the number of toilets. No more cold showers for the players or collapsing stands endangering the fans. The sharp contrast between the rickety old and fancy new ballparks is very apparent in New Britain, where the "Beehive," as the Rock Cats' obsolete former home was called, stands right behind the new $11-million facility opened by the city in 1996.

There also suddenly appeared a number of wealthy executives like Bill Dowling and Dan Burke, former chairman of Cap Cities/ABC and now owner of the Portland, Maine, Sea Dogs, who, frustrated by unfulfilled boyhood dreams of playing in the big leagues, seized on minor-league owner-ship as a retirement hobby. Most of the franchises have risen dramatically in value. "But behind the boom in minor-league baseball, there are also many broken dreams," a high school headmaster who moonlights as head usher for Burke's Sea Dogs told me. Consider the "players who won't ever make it to the Show and owners who thought there was a pot of gold at the end of the rainbow in center field."

Contributing most to the boom is the way small-town teams like the Rock Cats have learned to sell themselves with marketing and advertising campaigns that put the em-phasis on friendliness as well as on family fun. Before each game in New Britain, as happens in most minor-league parks, Little Leaguers swarm onto the field to take a bow, while a few designated players, including Liriano and Olson, canvass the crowd signing autographs. Sometimes it's hard to tell who is more thrilled, the players signing baseballs and scorecards or the awestruck little fans collecting them.

In Pawtucket's McCoy Stadium, because of the way the seats are arranged, the players are out of reach to the eager, young autograph seekers. Not to be denied, the kids have contrived to dangle baseballs on strings into the dugout like baited fishing lines, but with a pen attached for the players to sign with. During one game that I attended there, Red Sox right fielder Trot Nixon was rehabbing with the Paw-Sox. I counted 20 baseballs hanging in a row in front of the home team dugout for him to sign.

Everywhere, it seems, the games themselves are being embellished by a nonstop carnival of clowns, Sumo wres-tlers, clumsy mascots, dizzy bat races, and musical chairs—or, in New Britain, would you believe musical toilets! These oddball contests make what's being performed out on the diamond seem like it was inspired more by Walt Disney than Abner Doubleday. In fact, the entertainment part has become so crucial that Rochester Red Wings' General Manager Dan Mason refers to his job as "Director of Fun."

For youngsters, who have never seen such carryings-on in a big-league ballpark, the shows put on in the minors provide one captivating surprise after another. For that reason, many parents complain that at night games it's all they can do to drag the kids away after the seventh-inning stretch to put them to bed. For those who stay a fireworks show is often the grand finale.

The owners, managers, and coaches—the Dowling brothers and the Cliburn twins are prime examples—all work hard at endearing themselves to the community by appearing at high school games, Rotary meetings, and other civic events. Local business leaders are often invited to throw out the first ball. Tiny tots are escorted onto the field to run the bases, join in three-legged races, and other kiddie contests.

Some wealthy minor-league team owners who have bought their way into baseball as a hobby may not care if they operate at a loss. Not Bill Dowling. "We've paid our investors a dividend every year," he announced proudly. "And in 2004, would you believe, we grossed more than $4.4 million."

But Bill admitted that turning a profit in minor-league baseball doesn't come easy. "You have to have an edge in this business," he said. "So we worked out a marketing strat-

egy based on the demographics of the Hartford area. Some
1.5 million people live here, many of them in wealthy suburbs."

He, unlike many of the other owners, aimed the Rock
Cats' marketing strategy at the wives, not the husbands, even
though men are usually more rabid baseball fans. "It's my
belief," he said, "that the women of the world drive the hab-
its of the family. So when we bought the team I said, 'Let's
do something that appeals to the ladies.' We made a ballerina
into a mascot, but put a baseball bat in her hands. We adver-
tised on Nickelodeon, Oprah's show, and other programs
that mothers and kids watch. At the same time we took our
print ads out of the sports sections and put them in the life-
style and news sections. We also dressed up the stadium and
lowered our prices for everything including tickets."

Bill was on a roll describing all the innovations they'd
made to pull in women. His wife, Susan, whom he admitted
is not a baseball fan, even contributed some of the ideas.
Then, breaking his train of thought, he suddenly asked me:
"Do you know what a season ticket for a box seat at Yankee
Stadium costs? Eight thousand dollars, for the same seat we
charge 600 . . . It's the gals who watch their pennies, and
they appreciate how little it costs to go to a game here. You
can't fool them by just selling cheap bleacher tickets, and
jacking up the price of everything else.

"Do I sound like P.T. Barnum?" he asked.

3

LEGENDS TO BUILD ON

Teams in the minors, like those in the majors, create their own crop of legends, and the Rock Cats are no exception. Enhancing the popularity of baseball in New Britain, I discovered, are numerous unforgettable tales harking back to the original professional team organized there in 1884.

At first it didn't appear that anybody would be willing to take on the job of running the club. The city fathers tried to persuade businessman Thomas J. Lynch to be manager, but he opted to become an umpire instead and eventually served as president of the National League. As a last resort they turned to local attorney Henry C. Gussman, who agreed to do it on condition that he could also play second base.

On April 29, 1884, the brand-new team, called the New

Britains, opened its season against the Buffalo Bisons before some 600 cheering supporters who paid $5 each for season tickets. Gussman, who had spent practically all of his time arguing cases in courtrooms and very little time on baseball diamonds, committed five errors as the Bisons pounded the home team 28 to 1. The *Hartford Telegram* promptly demanded that "the manager appoint anybody but himself to play second base."

There were other problems. Electric Field (although it had no lights), where the New Britains played their home games, was owned by the local streetcar company. Unfortunately, the trolley line didn't extend that far, making it difficult to reach. Fans had to hitch up their horses or ride bicycles to get there. So professional baseball in New Britain got off to a poorly attended start, a situation that continued for years.

The team changed its name and venue several times until 1908, when it returned home as the Perfectos, named after the famous Havana cigar in deference to its four imported Cuban stars. One of them, the fleet-footed Armando Marsans, later became the first Hispanic to have a successful career in the majors, playing for the Cincinnati Reds, St. Louis Browns, and New York Yankees. Half black, he was nevertheless light-skinned enough to cross the big-leagues' rigid color barrier, a barrier that remained strong until Jackie Robinson joined the Brooklyn Dodgers. Reporters cited Marsans for his "audacious base running," describing his slides as "a thing of beauty." The records aren't clear, but some say that one year he was second only to Ty Cobb in stolen bases. His greatest achievement, though, was getting four base hits in one game off Giants great Christy Mathewson.

Ken Lipshez, a current sports reporter for the *New Britain Herald*, and a walking encyclopedia of local baseball lore, told me about one famous Perfectos game after which the umpire barely escaped being beaten to a pulp by New Britain's rabid fans. Apparently he allowed a tie game with New Haven that should have been called because of darkness to continue on into the evening. The pitchers had no trouble finding the plate, but the batters were swinging wildly in the gathering gloom.

A couple of innings later, two New Haven hitters did finally connect, sending what should have been a couple of routine fly balls soaring up into the darkness. The outfielders could hear the crack of the bat, but couldn't follow the flight of the balls that dropped in for doubles, giving New Haven a one-run victory.

Like a swarm of angry bees, the fans chased the ump under the grandstand and were about to grab him when he locked himself in the peanut vendor's stand, where he spent the night. But not even the Perfectos, with its Cuban stars, could make a go of it in New Britain.

Early in the 1912 season, the team relocated in nearby Waterbury and was renamed the Spuds after the surrounding potato fields. Another New Britain team known as the Sinks—named as far as anybody knows after a local manufacturer of bathroom and kitchen equipment—took its place in 1914. But the Sinks' 27-97 record that year proved embarrassing enough to keep professional baseball out of New

Britain for almost 70 years. Finally, the Boston Red Sox established their Double-A farm team there in 1983. Twelve years later the Minnesota Twins took over the franchise, renaming the team the Rock Cats.

According to pitching coach Stew Cliburn, New Britain's most legendary hometown player was an undersized, nearsighted, boozing pitcher named Steve Dalkowski, who old-timers claim made Olson's and Liriano's bullets look like mere puffballs. Although he grew up in New Britain, and now as a recovering alcoholic is spending his final years in a nursing home there, he never pitched professionally for the home team. But in 1957 all 16 major league teams had scouts in the stands when Steve, a New Britain high school senior, set a state record that still stands by striking out 24 batters in one game. Local fans also recall that his catcher and classmate Andy Baylock, who became baseball coach at the University of Connecticut, used to put a beefsteak in his mitt to soften the jarring impact of Steve's pitches.

Stew knows Dalkowski and occasionally invites him over to regale the Rock Cats with his wild tales. As the pitching coach tells it, Earl Weaver, Bobby Cox, and a few other former big-league managers who saw Steve in his prime, called him the "hardest throwing pitcher ever." His super-bullets were attributed to a very strong left wrist that gave the ball a hard snap as it flew from his fingers.

Dalkowski's renown spread far beyond New Britain. *Sports Illustrated* became so intrigued with the stories about him that it ran a nostalgic article about his super-fastball in its June 30, 2003, issue. The magazine reported that "When his left hand released a pitch, the ball took off with stunning speed rising like the jet stream." It also described how one day during spring training, Ted Williams was hanging around a batting cage where Dalkowski was warming up. The Red Sox star wanted to see for himself what the kid had. He let one pitch fly by, then stepped out of the cage, muttering that he hadn't even seen the ball.

Of course, as Stew pointed out, there were no radar guns in Dalkowski's day to verify his speed, but estimates ranged from 100 to 110 mph. The fact that one of his wild pitches knocked an umpire out cold reinforces those estimates. And so did a demonstration he put on for the benefit of disbelievers, hurling a baseball clean through a split-rail fence.

But because of his wildness, both on the field and in saloons off the field, Dalkowski's entire professional career (1957–1965) was confined to the minors. His one big chance came during a big-league tryout with the Baltimore Orioles, but it ended sadly for him with a blown-out elbow. While the stories about Dalkowski are still being argued in New Britain today, his minor-league statistics are irrefutable: In 995 innings he struck out 1,396 batters. But the wild man also walked 1,354 and ended his career with a not very impressive 5.59 earned run average.

New Britain also has a number of modern-day legends to reminisce about. Many of them are pictured on posters adorning the Rock Cats' clubhouse walls, put there by manager Stan Cliburn for the young aspirants like Olson and Liriano to take inspiration from. But none of their careers can match the color and drama of Dalkowski's, even though these players are currently experiencing considerably more success than he did. Included among them are Twins' short-

stop Jason Bartlett, third baseman Michael Cuddyer, outfielder Lew Ford, outfielder Torii Hunter, right-handed
pitcher Kyle Lohse, catcher Joe Mauer, and first baseman
Justin Morneau—all former Rock Cats stars and graduates of
what is regarded as the best farm system in the major leagues.

That isn't just my personal opinion. I read in the 2004
issue of *Baseball America*, the bible of the sport, that the Twins
were voted the best organization in baseball. And General
Manager Terry Ryan, who masterminded the team's extraordinary three-year back-to-back streak of American
League Central Division championships from 2002–2004,
was given the magazine's Executive of the Year award. I
gathered that his feat was considered remarkable because the
Twins' entire player payroll, including the salaries of all its
farmhands, was just a million dollars more than the $56 mil-
lion the Mets paid to sign pitcher Pedro Martinez, and min-
iscule compared to the $208 million the Yankees forked out
to its players in 2005.

In addition to Ryan's personal citation, *Baseball America*
also presented the Twins with its Organization of the Year
award based on "major-league performance, minor-league
affiliate direction, talent level throughout the system, quality
of player procurement, and overall direction." Although no
individual was named, that accolade, I assumed, was aimed
primarily at Jim Rantz, the Twins' minor-league director.

A burly, plainspoken Midwesterner, Rantz told me he
was signed by the Washington Senators (before the franchise
moved to Minnesota) when he was 21. He spent three years
in Triple-A and made it to the Senators' major-league spring

training camp. But like many young pitchers trying too hard to impress his coaches, he came down with a sore arm. And as he says, "Back in those days, if cortisone didn't work, you were out the door. Today they do various kinds of surgery and other wonderful things to preserve a pitcher's arm."

Finished as a player, he then managed the St. Cloud rookie club in the Northern League for one year. "I don't like to brag," he says, "but we won the pennant by 12 games. That's when I moved into the Twins' front office where I've been for the past 40 years." Then breaking into a broad grin, he adds, "Yes, I've seen a few balls and strikes."

Rantz was the first person I went to see at the Twins' training camp in Fort Myers last spring. The place was a hive of activity. Located in the Lee County Sports Complex, four diamonds and two auxiliary fields are situated around Hammond Stadium, home of the Fort Myers Miracle. All of the fields had practice games going on. The crack of bats and plunk of balls smacking into mitts filled the air as baseballs seemed to be flying in every direction.

A tower located between two of the diamonds enabled the coaches to follow the two most important practice games simultaneously, a dizzying task that seemed to me would leave them cross-eyed. It was hard enough just to tell the rookies from their major-league brothers because most of the players were dressed alike.

With the teams about to move north, Rantz was caught up in one meeting after another, trying to sort out who would play where once the regular season began. And of course who would be cut loose and declared free agents. He also had a very protective secretary, brought down from Minneapolis, who made it even more difficult to get to him. Finally, before breaking camp, he invited me in for a chat.

My main interest in interviewing him was to see if he thought I'd picked the right two pitchers, Liriano and Olson, both good prospects, but with vastly different backgrounds, to follow throughout the 2005 season. I knew he'd assigned them to the Rock Cats, and even though it was only a Double-A team, it had the reputation for sending quite a few of its players directly to the Twins. In fact, I was told that in the year 2000, seven Rock Cats made that leap. I also realized that Liriano had a leg up on Olson, having already been named to the Twins' 40-man roster. But not having been so designated didn't rule out Olson's chances of making it to Minneapolis, even if it took him more time.

Rantz, as might be expected, was noncommittal, reluctant to show any favoritism. "We draft young players and then promote them from within," is all he would say, indicating that both pitchers had the opportunity to move up the Twins' ladder. "We always try to develop our own players rather than acquiring them from other organizations."

My question gave the minor-league director the chance to express his cynicism about the Yankees, whom he claims "are always buying established stars like Jason Giambi, Randy Johnson, and Alex Rodriguez and then disposing of a number of the really good players they've nursed through their own farm system.

"Take a look," Jim adds, peering over his wire-rimmed spectacles, which make him appear more like a college professor than a baseball executive. "You'll find many big-leaguers on other teams who grew up in the Yankees organization."

Liriano and Olson, however, are exceptions to Rantz's promoting-from-within rule. Both were obtained from other teams. Liriano was acquired by what is called a "toss-in" to sweeten the deal with the San Francisco Giants in 2003, by which the Twins obtained pitchers Joe Nathan and Boof Bonser, both at the time considered a lot more promising than Liriano.

The Dominican had first caught the attention of scout Rick Ragazzo in a tryout camp on his native island. Signed in 2000 at the age of 16, he won five games and lost four in the rookie-level Arizona League the next year. But owing to recurring elbow and shoulder strain, he spent most of 2002 and 2003 on the disabled list, making him damaged goods when the Giants traded him. "I was very sad," he told reporters at the time. "I wanted to stay with the Giants."

With his left arm healed, he started the 2004 season with the Fort Myers Miracle, where he had an undistinguished 6-7 win-loss record and a 4.0 earned run average. But he'd also fanned 125 batters in 117 innings. That August, mainly because of his exceptional strikeout record, Jim Rantz promoted him to the Rock Cats, where he whiffed 49 more batters mainly with his overpowering fastball.

Olson was discovered by Twins' scout Billy Milos when he was pitching for the independent Rockford River Hawks in 2003. Assigned first to the Quad City River Bandits, Olson was soon moved up a notch in midseason to the Fort Myers Miracle. The next year working mainly out of the bull pen, he registered three consecutive saves in one week, led the team in wins with 7 in 45 games, while recording 85 strikeouts in 78 innings. His ERA (earned run average) of 2.88 was considerably better than Liriano's. Both pitchers were picked to play in the Florida State League All-Star Game. And certainly both looked upon the coming year with the Rock Cats as one more step up in their climb to the majors.

All in all, I came back from Fort Myers convinced I'd selected two worthy prospects for my book. The fact that they'd be sharing the same mound in New Britain, but as competitors as well as teammates, struck me as the makings of a potentially exciting story.

CALL FROM JIM RANTZ

The drive up historic Route 9 from Long Island Sound through the Connecticut River Valley to New Britain is one of the prettiest in all New England. The highway and its offshoots pass by the old whaling village of Essex, restored to its original quaint charm; the ornate Gillette Castle, built by former actor William Gillette as his private residence, but now a popular tourist attraction; the venerable Goodspeed Opera House, fully refurbished, and the home of many Broadway tryouts; the manicured campus of Wesleyan University; and finally the city of New Britain itself, a tight-knit community of former German and Polish immigrants.

On this sun-drenched morning of June 17, 2005, four days before summer, the oaks and maples enclosing the macadam highway are as thick and green as they ever get. For the Rock Cats, who have started the season with a dismal losing streak, the date also marks the beginning of an important seven-day home stand against the Altoona Curve, a Pirate farm, and the Binghamton Mets. These games, I hope, will provide a good opportunity to see both Liriano and Olson in action. In any case, if New Britain doesn't show some life in this series, it will be mired even deeper in the Eastern League cellar, a situation that so far, at least, hasn't discouraged the Rock Cats' fans, whose loyalty seems unswerving.

Like the rapid expansion of minor-league baseball, the New Britain community is going through something of a renaissance. A century ago it was known as the "Hardware City" of America, though since then it has lost most of that industry to the South, and to outsourcing abroad. For that reason the town clings tenaciously to its biggest remaining employer, the world-famous manufacturer of Stanley Tools, founded there in 1843.

The company, with 1,000 workers, is the Rock Cats' biggest supporter, its advertisements being very much in evidence around the stadium. The name "STANLEY" dominates the large illuminated scoreboard in center field. A yellow billboard with a picture of a Stanley hammer proclaiming: "HIT IT HARD" is located atop the right-field fence just inside the foul pole. Another billboard picturing a Stanley steel tape measure advising: "HIT IT LONG" sits atop the fence inside the left-field foul pole. The trouble with the Rock Cats so far this season is the team's batters are not hitting the ball either hard or long, much to the exasperation of manager Stan Cliburn and hitting coach Floyd Rayford. But that doesn't seem to be putting a dent in attendance.

The city, itself, has not been so lucky in attracting new enterprises, despite concerted efforts to spruce up the downtown shopping and restaurant district. At the same time the outlying area has started to reach out to high-tech firms by establishing something called "SMART" (Shared Manufacturing Area for Regional Technology) that the Chamber of Commerce claims is "shovel ready to grow your business."

Nobody ever thought of New Britain as a mecca for culture, but its Museum of American Art is gaining national attention for having one of the foremost collections of artwork depicting both historical and modern scenes in the United States—paintings by Thomas Cole, Albert Bierstadt, and John Frederick Kensett of the Hudson River School, Winslow Homer, John Singer Sargent, and Mary Cassatt—even one by Paul Sample, whom I studied drawing with at Dartmouth College. To accommodate its expanding collection, an impressive new building is going up next to the present old, wood structure.

We had already paid a visit to the museum in deference to my wife Helen, an artist, who is bored by baseball and believes the game would benefit by being limited to seven innings (as it is in all minor-league doubleheaders). She'd already sat patiently through enough Rock Cats' encounters that now when General Manager Bill Dowling sees her, he calls out, "How's St. Helen doing today?" To relieve the boredom she began sketching the various ballparks we attended starting down in Fort Myers. By the end of the season, I suspect she will have the best, if not the one-and-only, collection of pen-and-pencil renderings of minor-league baseball stadiums located in the eastern half of the United States.

Aside from the museum, one of New Britain's proudest municipal assets is its state-of-the-art baseball stadium, which it leases to the Rock Cats. The stadium is a miniature replica of the Baltimore Orioles' Camden Yards. Eight hundred seats were added this spring, so the ballpark now accommodates almost 7,500 fans; a good thing because many of the games are sellouts. The team is already well on the way to breaking its 2004 attendance record of 311,671, a remarkable turnout for a city with a population of only 71,538. But then the team is blessed with being a baseball monopoly. Nearby Hartford, which had once obtained a National Hockey League franchise, the Whalers, tried, but failed, to obtain a major-league baseball franchise, leaving fans there with no alternative but to drive the 20 miles to New Britain to satisfy their baseball craving.

Continuing north along picturesque Route 9, heading for exit 24, and Willow Brook Park where the stadium is located, I began drafting questions in my mind to ask Olson and Liriano. Back in Fort Myers during spring training, it was difficult pulling the players aside for interviews. They were too busy getting themselves into condition and competing for Single-A, Double-A, and Triple-A spots in the Twins' farm system. And on my Memorial Day visit to New Britain, getting plugged in with the Rock Cats' management, particularly the Cliburn twins and the Dowling brothers, didn't leave much time for mingling with the players.

All I had were a couple of quick conversations with Olson in the clubhouse while he was either suiting up or taking off his uniform and a brief talk with Liriano in the dugout, the day after the deluge washed out the game he started against the New Hampshire Fisher Cats.

Relaxed, good-natured, and strikingly handsome, Olson had impressed me as an all-American boy. His love of baseball and his big-league aspirations colored all of his comments. Modesty, I discovered, was going to be the only inhibiting factor for getting into the head of this young pitcher to find out what he considers are his successes and failures as the season progresses. He made it sound as if he had achieved Double-A status simply because of a few lucky breaks, not because of hard work and a strong right arm.

Liriano, I discovered, was either terribly shy or so elusive that *New Britain Herald* reporter Ken Lipshez had given up trying to wring a few quotes from him. In either case he was hard to corner in the clubhouse. As soon as he dressed for practice, he'd race out onto the field to run laps and do stretching exercises. And during those games he wasn't pitching, he often chose to sit in the grandstand alone, behind home plate, charting the opposing batters he would face during his turn on the rotation. But from my one brief conversation with him, I was relieved to discover he was reasonably fluent in English, though so reticent it was hard to extract more than a "yes" or "no." In the future, I decided, I was going to have to keep peppering away with the same basic question, but take different approaches, if I was ever going to succeed in delving into his thoughts. Otherwise I was going to have to rely almost entirely on what the manager and pitching coach had to say about how he reacted to different situations out on the mound.

Both Stan and his twin brother Stew had been very cooperative, sitting still for long tape-recorded interviews, explaining the strengths and weaknesses of the two pitchers. So I was counting on them to be my close allies for getting to Liriano as the season progressed.

My only problem was telling the manager and pitching coach apart. At least before, the identical twins—both with the same coppery hair and neatly trimmed mustaches—had donned their uniforms, Stan's with number 16 on the back and Stew's with number 33. The ballpark's souvenir concessionaire, I discovered, was capitalizing on the confusion these look-alikes caused. One of their best-selling items was a bobble-head doll with Stan's face on one side of the head and Stew's face on the other.

Their careers leading up to New Britain, however, had taken different paths. Stan became a catcher and Stew a pitcher. "Our high school coach in Jackson, Mississippi," Stan explained, "promised me that being a catcher was the fastest way to the majors, and I took him seriously. But he also warned me that the mask, chest-protector, and shin guards worn by catchers are called 'tools of ignorance' because of the physical beating taken by those stupid enough to train for that position."

Today, Stan claims that being a catcher helped prepare him for being a team manager. "After all, when you're crouched behind home plate, the whole game is out in front of you. You're like the field general or quarterback directing the action."

Being the better storyteller of the two, Stew relishes describing the first time he and Stan faced each other in a pro game. "It was 1979," he explains, "and I was pitching for the Portland (Oregon) Beavers, a Pittsburgh Pirates' farm club while Stan was catching for the Salt Lake City Gulls, a California Angels' farm. The game was being hyped by the local media as the 'Battle of the Twins.' We both knew it was going to be fun. Stan would come to bat swinging as hard as he could, trying to hit a home run. And I would throw as hard as I could, trying to strike him out.

"So what do you think happened? Stan popped up my first pitch to the first baseman and it was over like that."

Then in 1984 they faced each other again in a Pacific Coast League championship game. "This time," Stew explains, "I was pitching for the Edmonton Trappers, and Stan catching for the Hawaii Islanders. We were ahead by one run in the ninth, but the Islanders had a man on first when the game came down to the final out with Stan at bat. You know what happened this time?" chortles Stew, still enjoying the opportunity to tell a story I'm certain he'd told many times before, "Damned if I didn't strike him out."

After a five-year major-league career as a relief pitcher for the Angels and some time coaching in Venezuela, Stew finally ended up as pitching coach for the Rock Cats in 1999. Stan, who also played briefly for the Angels, didn't become New Britain's manager until 2001. Nevertheless, Stew recognizes his brother as boss. "After all, Stan's two-and-a-half minutes older," he says. "There's absolutely no sibling rivalry," claims Bill Dowling. "They complement each other beautifully. I'd hate to see either of them leave."

On my previous visit to New Britain, Stew had expressed great admiration for Liriano, claiming he was one of the best prospects he'd ever encountered in the minors. "He's very coachable. He retains information very well. And he's open to suggestions," Stew declared. "Sure, we had to do a few mechanical things, but not much." The pitching coach then went on to give me a complete appraisal of the 21-year-old's extraordinary ability.

"This guy lights up the radar gun with 92- to 97-mile-an-hour fastballs. He averages 94. That, according to the Twins' rating system, is what we call a seven fastball on a scale of two to eight. And so it goes, down the line. A number six fastball averages 92 to 93 miles an hour, a number five, 89 to 91, a number four, 87 to 88, a number three, 85 to 87, and a number two, 82 to 84. If you get a guy averaging 96, that's an eight, but there aren't many of those around, since the scoring's based on what a guy throws on average during the whole game, not just for one or two pitches. So Liriano's almost on the top of the ladder with his fastball."

Stew didn't stop there. He wanted to make sure I realized just how exceptional Liriano is. "For a young man his age, he's also got a devastating changeup. So after his changeup, his fastball probably looks to the hitter like it's coming in at 100 miles an hour. And he throws the changeup for strikes the same way Johan Santana does. Many big-league pitchers don't know how to keep hitters off balance that way."

I could see that Stew was determined to go through Liriano's entire arsenal of pitches. "Actually, he's got two different changeups," he explained, "both thrown with the same arm action as his fastball. One drops straight down, and the other breaks away from right handers. But I still think his best pitch is his wipeout 87-mile-an-hour slider."

The pitching coach couldn't seem to find enough praise for the Dominican's natural ability. "It's very unusual to see a kid coming up with that many quality pitches. But sometimes he forgets he has them and goes out there knowing he can throw his fastball past the guy and gets out of his element."

Stew hesitated for a moment, trying to recall which game it was. "Oh, yeah," he said, "it was in his first start against Norwich last month. He tried to blow the ball by everybody for the first three innings, forgetting that their guys were from his old San Francisco Giants' organization and were probably geared up for him. They got ten hits and five runs off him in six innings. You see, he still has to learn to use a little baseball savvy, a little strategy, by sticking to his mechanics and not trying to overthrow so he's missing his spot, and the ball's up in the zone, and all over the place."

Obviously, the pitching coach didn't want me to go away thinking that he wasn't doing anything to correct these deficiencies. "We also had to teach him to go out there and pitch instead of just going out there and throwing," continued Stew. "Now he's hitting the mitt where the ball needs to go on the outside and inside corners.

"Another thing we worked on is his stride. We've gotten him to throw more across his body. Not a lot, but a little bit for incseased deception. All left-handed pitchers have a tendency to do that, but when they don't do it correctly, or too much, they have a tendency to 'open the gate,' as we call it, and end up with their legs spread too far apart after releasing the ball."

Stew proceeded to demonstrate what he meant by standing up and extending his right leg to one side. "In that position," he explained, "pitchers lose the advantage of their own full height and the height of the mound. They're no longer throwing the ball down hill. Right-handed pitchers tend to throw straight on, so it's not as much of a problem for them." It was beginning to look like Stew had given Liriano a whole checklist of things to review before he even threw a pitch.

Still, the pitching coach wasn't finished. "We also had to make sure that Liriano's arm slot, as I call it, is in the 'L' position." Again Stew demonstrated what he meant by crooking his arm to form an "L." "That way he keeps his fingers on top of the ball and pitches on a down angle. He's adjusted to that very well, and hopefully it will keep him from having the elbow and shoulder problems he had a couple of years ago."

But Stew didn't think a recurrence was likely. "Obviously, he's gotten stronger since then. He's got a nice, lean pitcher's body, and he's flexible. A lot of times pitchers get into professional ball not realizing they've got to get their bodies in shape and their mechanics right so they can go out there and throw every fifth day."

I gathered that Stew figured he might have extended Liriano's career by altering his mechanics. "We think the delivery he has now will make him injury free," he declared. "But we still have to be careful. We have a pitch limit for all our starters. We tried not to let them throw more than 85 to

100 pitches up until May 15. Then we raised the limit to 110."

It had been great for me getting that advance briefing on Liriano's strengths and weaknesses. But because the Dominican had been so hard for me to pin down, I decide to telephone Stew from the car and ask if he could set up an appointment with him for me. I call the Super 8 Motel in Cromwell, where Stan and Stew stay during the Rock Cats' 72 home games. It's a clean, no-frills, inexpensive establishment that offers orange juice, freshly brewed coffee, and muffins for breakfast, an attraction that was bringing my wife and me back for the second time. It's also just a 10-minute drive from the ballpark and a block away from the Cromwell Diner, a full-scale, 24-hour restaurant where it's possible to enjoy a late dinner after the night games.

The clerk at the Super 8 reports that both Cliburns have already left for the ballpark. That seems strange since it is still morning, and practice for the night games doesn't start until around 3 PM. So I call Bill Dowling, whom I know will be reachable at his stadium office. But his assistant, John Willi, reports that he is closeted in a meeting with Stan and Stew.

Something's going on, I think. Not that emergency, closed-door meetings are anything unusual for this team, stuck deep in the Eastern League basement. In fact, the joke making the rounds of the press box claims that the Rock Cats, already 13 games under 500, and 12 games behind division-leader Portland, are leading the league in meetings.

As a last resort I call Jeff Dooley, the Rock Cats' play-by-play radio broadcaster. He always seems to know what's going on. "Better get up here in a hurry," he announces in his resonant radio voice, suddenly ending my idyllic drive up the Connecticut River Valley. "Liriano's just been called up to Rochester. And he's leaving for the airport right after lunch."

5

A STAR IS LOST

When I arrived at the clubhouse all the Latinos were jubilantly huddled around their departing pal, Liriano: catchers Jose Morales and Gabby Torres, first baseman Danny Matienzo, designated hitter Luis Jimenez, left-fielder Alex Romero, and second baseman Gil Velazquez, the core of the starting lineup. Apparently they'd taken Liriano to lunch at some nearby restaurant, perhaps even celebrating with a beer or two, and were now in the process of wishing him well on his next step up the ladder.

I couldn't believe how laid back and lacking in emotion Liriano looked. He had always struck me as a pretty cool character. But with this unexpected call-up, I expected he'd be hard-pressed to contain his excitement. Yet, from all outward appearances he might just as well have been demoted to Fort Myers. Perhaps he's sad saying good-bye to buddies, I thought, even though they failed miserably to back him up with hits when he was pitching. Or maybe, he's unhappy leaving behind such a disappointing record.

In his 13 starts Liriano had managed only three wins against five defeats. Trainer Chad Jackson thought the cold weather in April, May, and June might have affected his throwing. In fact, on June 10, in what turned out to be his last game for the Rock Cats, and one of his best, he began grimacing noticeably in the sixth inning, after having struck out nine Trenton batters.

"I could tell he was shying from using his slider," Stew Cliburn explained. "That's a sign of muscle fatigue." Stew said his decision to yank Liriano short of his allowed 110 pitches was based on the Twins' minor-league policy of removing any hurler showing shoulder or elbow pain, not because the Dominican suddenly gave up two hits and a pair of walks and appeared to be fading.

"Ordinarily, I'd have let him work himself out of a hole like that," Stew claimed. But he also announced that the Dominican would miss his next turn in the rotation, indicating that he might have actually done some damage to his arm. Of course, that was before the Rock Cats' pitching coach knew his star protégé was headed for Rochester.

Obviously, what had caught the eye of Jim Rantz, boss of the Twins' minor-league operations and the man responsible for Liriano's promotion, were the 92 strikeouts he'd racked up in just 76-and-1/3 innings. Besides his explosive fastball, the young pitcher had also demonstrated fair control, having issued only 26 walks. Even so, Rantz's decision to send him up to Rochester hit like a sledgehammer, not only in the clubhouse, but also in the Rock Cats' front office. Bill Dowling could count on an extra 500 or 600 fans showing up on the days the Dominican was scheduled to pitch.

Just before Liriano stepped into the white van with a large scowling rock cat painted on its side, I was able to catch a few moments with him alone. None of the local reporters had arrived yet to cover the game that night. They probably would have had a barrage of questions to throw at the elusive lefty. But coming face to face with him so unexpectedly, I felt stupidly unprepared with any of my own. "Have you telephoned your parents in San Cristobal with the good news?" I asked lamely, racking my mind for a more probing question to ask at this crucial moment in his career. "Will they come to Rochester to see you pitch?"

Instantly, I realized how unlikely that was. How could his mother and father obtain visas with the heightened security imposed after September 11? As the Latin players themselves admit, "The only way to get to America from the Caribbean now is to bat or pitch your way off one of the islands."

Nevertheless, my question seemed to break the tension of his leaving. The broad, bronzed face, frizzed with short curly black hair, flashed a big smile, the first I could recall ever seeing on the face of this solemn young man.

"Yes, I called them last night," he answered softly, with only a slight accent. "They were very happy." That also was a more complete response than I had gotten from him previously. Could it be that the sudden promotion to Triple-A was loosening Liriano up? If so, that would surely bode well for the future.

He also seemed pleased when I mentioned that I'd be coming up to Rochester to see him pitch, although I had no idea how I was going to cover the Red Wings and Rock Cats at the same time. Even so, Liriano's unexpected good news was having a vicariously uplifting effect on me as well. I felt elated that my preseason prediction seemed to be coming true, that this talented pitcher was destined for the big leagues. And there I was face to face with him as he was about to take the first big step in that direction.

In a few minutes the white van with Liriano and all his gear packed in it rolled out of the stadium parking lot headed for the Hartford airport, leaving me to ponder seriously how I was going to keep up with both him and Olson. Not only would they now be pitching for different teams, but in different leagues. Rochester and the rest of the International League clubs were spread over a much wider territory, extending from Indianapolis and Louisville in the Midwest, to Richmond and Durham in the South, and even reaching up to Ottawa in Canada. Even more difficult at the moment was deciding how to break the news to Helen that she was going to be sitting through many more baseball games in many more ballparks than I'd anticipated—and with many miles and long hours in the car between them.

The players started filtering into the clubhouse, some stopping first in the training room, a tableaux of rippling muscles under black-and-white skins, to work out on the exercise machines. Others headed straight for their lockers, while a few just plunked themselves down on the big leather couch in front of the large-screen TV set to watch ESPN's coverage of the College World Series. Minor-league players, it seems, never get tired of watching other teams play baseball. Perhaps they consider it educational.

The stunning news of Liriano's promotion had already reached most of them. Manager Stan Cliburn, it turned out, had received the call from Jim Rantz in Minneapolis the night before, and immediately relayed the good news to Liriano, who probably phoned a few of his buddies. The jungle telegraph in organized baseball works as fast as it does in the corporate world. Still, the loss of the team's star pitcher was causing quite a buzz as the players suited up for practice.

"Who will take Liriano's place on the rotation?" That was of greatest concern. Jim Abbott, the big right-hander from Caledonia, Michigan, and Justin Olson's roommate, appeared to be the rumor mill's choice, even though he had proved ineffective as a reliever. In 12 starts he'd given up 36 hits in 26-and-2/3 innings. But this was Abbott's third year with the Rock Cats, although he missed almost half the games in 2004 because of "Tommy John surgery" to repair a Labrum tear in his right shoulder. This also marked his sixth season in the minors. According to rules of professional baseball, if he failed to make the majors by 2006, he'd have to be released as a free agent. Then there was also the possibility of a starter with the Miracle being called up from Florida.

Olson, who came up to the Rock Cats as a starter, was an outside possibility. However, he told me on my last trip to New Britain that he'd become accustomed to pitching out of the bull pen, and felt very comfortable in that role.

Yet, on occasion when one of the regulars missed a turn, he'd been pressed into service as a so-called spot starter—and did pretty well. Of course, I was hoping it would be Olson. As soon as he showed up in the clubhouse, I pulled him aside for a chat.

"Liriano deserved it. I wasn't surprised," were the first words out of his mouth. But then Olson had always been generous in his praise for the Dominican. "The team didn't back him up with hits, but he pitched well," continued Justin, who also sounded genuinely sorry to see his teammate go. "We were good friends. Everybody liked Liriano."

In spite of this magnanimous reaction, Olson, a fierce competitor out on the field, had every right to feel a twinge of jealousy, perhaps even anger. Especially since he'd once told me that as a kid he was such a sore loser that his parents kept him from playing organized sports until he was 11 or 12 years old. But he showed no evidence of that now, although he'd already notched six victories compared to Liriano's three, and racked up 60 strikeouts while giving up only 28 walks in 72-and-2/3 innings—an impressive record for a pitcher who'd been alternating as starter and reliever. And his numbers would have been even better if during his last two starts on June 1 against the Norwich Navigators, and on June 13 against the Reading Phillies, his teammates hadn't booted several ground balls, presenting their opponents with a bunch of unearned runs.

In any case, Olson appeared in an expansive mood and eager to chat. We'd already established a pretty good relationship, although I'd never probed very deeply into how and why, after studying to be a teacher, he decided to embark on a professional baseball career. And more importantly, how at 25, a not-so-young age for a minor-league pitcher, he envisioned his future. Did he hope to break out of the bull pen? Did he, too, expect to be called up to Rochester this year? Did he ever really consider himself a big-league prospect the way the coaches seemed to regard Liriano? And what about now? Did he still retain that boyhood dream of making the Show?

During previous conversations I'd been struck by the young right-hander's disarming frankness. His answers to my questions had always been direct, sometimes even blunt. So I wasn't surprised when he told me right off, "On the day I discover there's no longer any possibility of my pitching in the big leagues, I'll quit playing baseball."

No, he didn't believe that his parents' decision to keep him from playing organized sports early on had proved a handicap. "In my freshman and sophomore years at Oak Park High School," he explained, "I was already pitching and playing a little infield. Then in my junior and senior years, I was just pitching. Our team was real good and the last year we made it all the way to the state finals."

The University of Illinois had been quick to offer Olson an athletic scholarship. Surprisingly, though, he finished college as an All–Big Ten academic star, while his mound performances didn't go all that well. "I got hurt halfway through my sophomore year," he explained. "I was a starter my junior year with a mediocre four-and-four record. But then in my senior year the coach moved me into the bull pen."

Olson figured he was done with baseball and took another year of college. He majored in kinesiology, an obscure subject that he described as "the study of anatomy in relation to body movements," which he planned to teach. "Of course I couldn't pitch in my fifth year," he said. "I went back and did a little coaching at Oak Park High. I also started throwing again, and my arm felt good. When none of the teaching jobs I applied for came through, I decided to try playing independent ball with the Rockford River Hawks. But just for one summer. It was only because I had nothing else to do. So I can't say it was always my dream to play in the majors."

For Stan and Stew Cliburn, Liriano's departure came as both a blow and a bouquet. They hated to lose him. But as Stew said, "It's a feather in our cap whenever the Twins reach down and grab one of our players for Triple-A." Even so, he wasn't in a good mood when I poked my head into his cramped office and waved my pocket tape recorder in his direction. He kept peering into the screen of his laptop containing all the records of his pitchers. It occurred to me that he still might be trying to decide on Liriano's replacement in the starting rotation. Reluctantly, he motioned me in and immediately eliminated any speculation about that.

"Jim Abbott's the legitimate guy to come in and start," Stew announced squelching my hope that it might be Olson. "We've had him in the bull pen this year. But he pitched in the rotation here last year and the year before. He'll be 26 in October. Here's our chance to see what he can do."

"What about Olson?" I asked, since I wasn't giving up on him as one of the two main characters for my book.

"Olson's back in his element, doing a great job in relief,"

Stew replied. "He's our best middle-innings guy. If our starter gets knocked out early, he can come in and give us four or five good innings."

That, I concluded, didn't mean Stew was down on Olson, or that his career had come to a dead end. Stew, in fact, made it clear that the Rock Cats would continue using Olson as a spot starter as well as in the bull pen. "We gave him his chance to start here and he did pretty good," Stew added. "But when we put him in the pen, he scored three wins in a row."

Once Stew got started, he didn't seem to want to let me go. "Liriano's promotion," he explained, "is going to be a tremendous challenge all 'round: for Abbott who's taking his place, and of course for the Dominican himself. Up in Rochester he's going to have to pitch finer and stop walking guys, though his control got better while he was here. But in Triple-A the batters are more disciplined. They don't swing at bad balls so much. That's why I kept telling Liriano, 'throw to hit the mitt. Don't try to miss the bat.' But I think he'll do well up there," Stew added somewhat skeptically, I thought. And then he launched into a monologue about how the major-league organizations are rushing their best young prospects too much.

"There are a lot of guys in the big leagues now who are still learning how to pitch," he said. "That's why you see all these inflated earned run averages. Twenty years ago when I was with the Angels, if you had a five or six ERA you were going to get optioned out. Money is another reason for rushing these kids. They can pay them four or five hundred thousand compared to the veteran guys that are making four or five million." Then as I started to leave, the pitching coach finally bared his disappointment. "I thought we'd get to keep Liriano at least until the Eastern League All-Star break."

Stan Cliburn's slightly less cramped office is just across the corridor from Stew's, and I was sure the manager had overheard his twin brother's last lament. "No, I wasn't surprised they took Liriano," Stan announced as soon as I clicked on my tape recorder. "This is a guy who's developed a lot. Look at his last outing. He gave up five hits, one run, and struck out nine in six innings before Stew thought maybe his shoulder was bothering him. And that was against Trenton with a couple of former Yankee hitters in the lineup. Sure, he's only three-and-five in the won-lost column, but he's pitched well enough to be seven-and-one."

Obviously, Stan didn't want me to go away thinking the twin brothers hadn't prepared Liriano adequately for his new assignment. "I think this is Jim Rantz's way of challenging the young man," he said. "He's looking down the line and sees Liriano as a guy who could help the major-league club. Don't be surprised if you see him in a Minnesota Twins uniform come September," was Stan's parting shot.

On the way out of the clubhouse I ran into Jeff Dooley, the Rock Cats' play-by-play radio announcer, who echoed the same thought. "Don't forget the kid's only 21. If he pitches well in Triple-A, the Twins will call him up on September 1st," Dooley assured me. "That's when the major-league rosters are expanded to 40 players. And technically Liriano's already on the 40-man roster, so he's got a better chance than most of being called up." Then Dooley went on to extol the virtues of a player remaining in Double-A. "This is a make-or-break league," he claimed. "It's a pretty good showcase for power, where the best prospects really stand out. Triple-A has more veterans, many with major-league time. This is a prospects' league."

Nevertheless Dooley wasn't too happy about the Dominican's "premature promotion," as he called it. "For selfish reasons as a broadcaster, I wish they'd left him here," he admitted. "All the fans know him and rooted for him whenever he pitched."

Since I was running around the ballpark getting everyone's reaction to Liriano's promotion, I couldn't very well exclude Bill Dowling, who'd just lost his biggest drawing card. I expected he'd be very upset having this happen so early in the season. Surprisingly, the jovial Irishman couldn't have been mellower. "That's minor-league baseball for you," he said. "The parent club doth giveth and it doth taketh away." Yet, Bill let me know that he'd already had a frank conversation that morning with Jim Rantz.

" 'Hey, Jim,' I said, 'we love each other but you're killing me. This is the worst thing. This is the one guy our fans really relate to who's going to end up in the big leagues. It's really bad for the franchise.' "

Bill then reminded me that the Twins' minor-league boss had done the same thing two years ago when he called up catcher Joe Mauer, the Rock Cats' best hitter, early in the season. "But Rantz is an understanding guy," Bill added. "He promised to send us a Triple-A pitcher to replace Liriano. And I told him, 'Hey, Jim, send us a couple of power hitters while you're at it.' "

The discussion about the loss of his star players started Bill reminiscing about his own career in baseball. "For three years from '96 to '98 I was general counsel for the Yankees, working right at the stadium," he said. "Then I left and became the team's outside lawyer for five more years. George (Steinbrenner) still always invites me for opening day. Unfortunately, this year we opened the same day, so I couldn't go."

After leaving the Yankees, Bill explained, he was determined to have a sports team of his own. "Coleman Levy, a local lawyer, and I made a bid to buy the Hartford Whalers' hockey team. It didn't work, so we both said, 'Let's see if we can buy a baseball team in this neck of the woods.' Joe Buzzas, a second baseman for the Yankees during World War II, owned a number of minor-league teams, including the New Britain Red Sox and the Salt Lake City Buzz.

"The Red Sox wanted to move the team to Springfield in 1995. Joe got mad and said, 'Take your affiliation outta here. I don't want it any more,' and signed with Minnesota. Joe was also tired of shuttling back and forth between New Britain and Salt Lake City. So Coleman and I lined up an investment group of about 20 people and bought the Rock Cats for $6.5 million. But we kept the controlling interest for ourselves, partly on the basis of sweat equity."

Bill and his partner also struck a good deal with the city for use of the stadium. The annual lease payments run about $90,000 a year. The Rock Cats also pay about 60 percent of the $100,000 utility costs, while the $3 parking fees return another $100,000 to the city. However, the New Britain Parks and Recreation Department keeps the playing field in beautiful condition and the stadium immaculately clean.

During the season, Bill still spends two days a week, sometimes three, at his law firm in New York City. He and his wife, Susan, have a home in Cobble Hill, Brooklyn, and another in East Haddam on the Connecticut River. But even when he's not at the ballpark he keeps close tabs on the team. "Any night I'm not there," he said, "I call in at 11:30 PM and get a recap of the game."

As diplomatically as I could, I asked if he ever got involved in the running of the team. "Not directly," he said. "Stan and Stew, they'll listen to me. Jim Rantz will ask me, do I like this player or that player, and do they move around the community, making appearances on radio or TV. Stan is really fabulous. He goes everywhere speaking and making friends for the team. He also wants to win. It's a very important part of his make-up. You've got to love a guy like that."

Bill Dowling also likes to win. Perhaps that's why he's too tense to ever sit down during a game. You can usually find him standing right behind section 108, just to the right of home plate. But he was also philosophic about his ball club's last-place standing, at least as it was on the day Liriano got whisked away. "Don't forget we're a development team," he added, echoing the words of the folks in Minneapolis that supply his players. "The stars like Liriano and Olson may come and go, pitching their hearts out, hoping to move up the ladder to Rochester, and then on to the big leagues."

But it was easy to tell that didn't stop Bill Dowling from loving his job. "This is wonderful," he said. "It's every kid's dream."

6

THE "MIDDLE-INNINGS GUY"

Keeping current on my two pitchers, it became clear, would require reliance in part on the Internet. Fortunately, Rochester's website, Redwingsbaseball.com, and New Britain's Rockcats.com provided detailed daily coverage of each team. So while I was still in New Britain covering Olson, I discovered Liriano had gotten off to a brilliant beginning in Triple-A.

In his first game on June 20 against Indianapolis, he pitched six innings, allowed only one hit, one earned run on a homer by former Mets' slugger Ty Wigginton, and struck out eight. Rochester went on to win 4 to 3, but only after stringing together four singles and scoring two runs in the top of the ninth when Liriano was no longer in the game, so he didn't get credit for the victory. Still, unlike the weak-hitting Rock Cats, the Red Wings were playing 500 ball, aided by several strong hitters who would surely help the Dominican improve his sickly win-loss record during the rest of the season.

Meanwhile back in New Britain, manager Stan Cliburn, frustrated by the lack of power in his lineup, was cheered by the arrival of Denard Span, a new leadoff batter brought up from the Miracle. Still, the manager kept hammering away to his players on the fundamentals of hitting, hoping it would result in more runs for Olson and the other hurlers. When I innocently wandered into his office on June 23 before a game with Binghamton, he started letting off steam by repeating his whole hitting-lecture to me.

"What I try to teach these guys is to be aggressive," he explained. "If you see a fastball in the strike zone, go get it. Don't just stand there. You might not see one again. If it's a tough breaking ball, hold off. That's a pitcher's pitch. But every at-bat, you're going to get a pitch to hit. It's just a matter of when you're going to take advantage of it." I'd heard him deliver different versions of that same spiel before. But he seemed eager to work off his frustrations. So I continued to tape what turned into a long monologue.

Stan said he realized it was a tough adjustment for his hitters going from Single-A to Double-A. "I had guys like Justin Morneau and Mike Cuddyer a couple of years ago that are doing well for Minnesota. They had trouble their first year here. It takes a while learning to hit better pitching."

But the manager still had hopes for the current season. "In 2003," he said, "we got off to a slow start. I told the guys if we win 20 games in August we'll be in the play-offs. We won the twentieth game on the last day, and that did it. In 2001 we won the Eastern League championship. That, too, was a team that started off slow. It all depends if you have a good August. This isn't a sprint. It's a marathon," he reminded me. Still, Stan left me thinking it would take a real miracle, not the one in Fort Myers, to pull his team out of its current slump.

The Rock Cats were still 13 games below the 500 mark on July 11 when Olson took the mound, filling in once again as a spot starter. "It was a morning game," Stan explained, "and nobody in the regular rotation was ready." This time Justin pitched brilliantly, beating the Bowie Baysox 2 to 1 on their home turf. In five quality innings, he allowed only two hits and one run while striking out six, the narrow victory gaining a split for New Britain in the finale of a four-game series. Even Stan, often quick to criticize Olson's mechanics and his proclivity for throwing home run balls, couldn't voice enough praise for his performance that day. "You know Olson's a bull pen guy. But he's really developing. This time he showed us that he can do it all."

That was the tall right-hander's 25th appearance of the season, 12 of them as a starter. The victory lifted his win-loss percentage to an even 500—seven victories and seven defeats, making him the team's leading pitcher. Even more important, his mastery of the Bowie batters seemed to have ignited the rest of the Rock Cats. The boys returned in high spirits from the Eastern League All-Star break and proceeded to take 10 of their next 13 games. "Olson changed our clubhouse chemistry," the manager admitted.

Stan had told me on several occasions what an avid believer he is in clubhouse chemistry. "Several years ago," he said, "I had a conversation with Sparky Anderson about the way he managed the Cincinnati Reds back in the seventies. He had all those egos to contend with: Pete Rose, Johnnie Bench, George Foster, and Tom Seaver. 'If I can control the chemistry in the locker room,' Sparky claimed, 'those guys get so pumped up, it's basically all over when I put 'em out in the field.'"

Stan claimed he could now feel the Rock Cats' spirit rising and was counting on their positive mood to continue through the second half of the season. "Look for yourself," he said. "You'll see the players are coming to the ballpark early and staying late because they want to talk to each other. Each guy wants to tell the other guy how well he's doing. They can't seem to soak up enough of the winning atmosphere."

Olson made his next start on July 18 against the Binghamton Mets. This time the Rock Cats' batters came alive, scoring 11 runs. Right-fielder Doug Deeds, New Britain's leading hitter, who came up from the Miracle with Olson, hit a two-run homer in the first inning, while shortstop Denard Span, the new leadoff batter, got three hits, including a two-run double in the second. So Olson didn't have to be so stingy with his hits and runs during what the *Hartford Courant* termed a "gritty performance." In six innings he gave up four runs—three earned—on six hits and two walks. But he struck out six with a searing fastball that the *Courant* also claimed had "plenty of late action."

Those two successive wins as a starter renewed Justin's

confidence, and just in time after a disastrous relief appearance in Norwich a week earlier. That dismal showing had come just when the Rock Cats looked like they were finally getting ready to leave last place. The night before they'd scored 14 runs in a blowout against the Navigators, continuing what was then a three-game winning streak.

Coming on in the fourth inning, Olson quickly induced the Navigators to hit into a double play, ending a two-run rally. But in the fifth inning, he loaded the bases and then walked the next three batters, allowing the Navigators to score five more runs and take a 7 to 0 lead. It was Olson's worst showing with the Rock Cats. In just 2-and-2/3 innings, he walked five and allowed five runs, while striking out only one. "I couldn't find the plate that night," he complained.

Stan Cliburn recognized his problem. "Olson started aiming the ball and pushing it up there instead of hitting the catcher's mitt," he explained. "He does that sometimes. But we let him go out and pitch the sixth, and I was glad to see him put a '0' up on the scoreboard. Sometimes we keep a pitcher in there just to see if he can't correct the problem himself." Apparently, Stan's confidence-building psychology worked.

On his next relief stint on July 25, Olson came through as was expected of him, snuffing out a rally by the league-leading Portland Sea Dogs. The Rock Cats held a 7 to 4 lead when he was called in with two outs and a man on first in the sixth inning. At first it looked like Olson was headed for yet another disaster when he walked the first two batters he faced, loading the bases. Then working up to a dangerous three-and-two count, he blew a fastball past Sea Dogs' slugger Brandon Moss to end the inning. The Rock Cats went on to win the game 9 to 4, extending their winning streak to nine in a row.

The next day Olson arrived at the ballpark early enough for me to sit down with him for a long interview. On a bench outside the entrance to the locker room, out of earshot of the other players, he confided his worries about his inconsistency. "I was flirting with danger last night in Portland when I walked those two batters in the sixth inning," he said. "It bothers me when I lose my concentration and do something like that."

Then he went on to describe how excited he was when the Twins moved him up to the Rock Cats this season. "This is a big year for me playing in Double-A," he said. "But I'm a little disappointed in the way I've been pitching. I'm not wholly discouraged, though what I saw in my head during the off-season was a lot better than my numbers are now." It occurred to me that he was comparing his own to Liriano's impressive numbers filtering down from Rochester. The Dominican had already won four games for the Red Wings, while losing only one. And his lone defeat to Durham was a result of five unearned runs.

As he rambled on, Olson acted pleased having me as a sounding board, although I tried hard not to interrupt his free-flowing conversation with my reactions. "I'm learning a lot," he continued. "Absolutely! I've got better command of my pitches and am now able to throw a curveball or a changeup in a fastball count. Just little improvements like that. Nothing big. Stew now calls me his middle-innings guy, and that makes me feel pretty good.

"Yes," he added, "Stew's been great, doing a little fine tuning on my mechanics. He's always positive and ready to help, just as pitching coach Eric Rasmussen was at the Miracle. Other than that, Stew lets you do your own thing. Of course, when he sees something wrong he tells you."

The conversation with Olson quickly veered off of baseball. There were many other things on his mind that he obviously felt like talking about—his marriage, his mother, and his father's early death during his sophomore year in college.

"My dad was head football coach at Oak Park High School, where I went," Justin explained. "He'd had heart surgery to replace his aorta valve, but came through it just great, probably because he was always big on fitness. One day he was walking out of the exercise room after working out on the stair-step machine. 'See you later!' he called out to a woman teacher also working out there. When she looked back Dad was crumpled up on the floor, dead from a massive heart attack.

"That happened during my sophomore year in college, and it changed my outlook as an athlete. As a coach Dad was a great believer in repetitive training. His death made me work harder to become a better pitcher. I often think of him when I'm warming up in the bull pen."

With his widowed mother still living in Illinois, I suspected Justin felt a little guilty playing baseball so far away. Especially when he explained that she was about to sell her home. In the off-season he worked as a house painter, and she was waiting for him to come back to brighten it up before putting it on the market. His wife, too, was back in Oak Park, and working as a paralegal in Chicago to help cover their expenses, so it was very difficult for them to find time together.

"Jamie and I got married two years ago," he said. "Even though the two of us are working, we're still trying to figure out how to save enough money to buy a house. I give pitching lessons in the off-season as well as painting. Painting in the winter is really a letdown, though the man I work for is a nice guy. He pays good money, and he always lets me come back to work for him during the off-season. Without that extra money we'd be in trouble."

That surprised me because I assumed the pay in Double-A, just two steps away from the big leagues, must be pretty good. And with half their time spent on the road, a substantial part of the players' expenses were paid. Justin quickly set me straight. "You see, in the first year in Double-A, we only get $1,700 a month, barely enough to cover our living expenses. On the road they pay for our hotel, but $20-a-day is all we get for food." His biggest expense in New Britain, he explained, is the two-bedroom apartment he shares with pitcher Jim Abbott, who is also married. "We need a place for our wives to stay when they come to visit."

I asked Olson a question that has always aroused my curiosity about relief pitchers. "What do you guys talk about out in the bull pen? Do you pass the time chatting about your families and the kind of personal stuff you just mentioned? Or are you too intent in following the game?"

"We don't sit there and talk about baseball all the time,"

he answered, laughing. "We'd drive ourselves crazy. Sometimes we even play some games." But he also pointed out that it's important to follow what's happening on the diamond pretty closely. "You need to see how the game's progressing. Everyone tries to figure out when and if he's going to be called. If the starter's doing well, you know he's going to throw six or seven innings. Then the set-up guy's going to be called in, and finally the closer. If the starter's struggling by the third or fourth inning, that's when I start stretching and getting ready."

Justin finally got around to discussing his future. He seemed to be looking at it with a pretty cold eye. "I plan to make a career out of baseball," he said. "If eventually things don't work out, and by work out I mean getting to the majors, then I'll go back to teaching. I've got my college degree in kinesiology, so this is all sort of a bonus."

I wondered what his reaction would be if Jim Rantz sent him back to pitch for the Rock Cats a second year. "Sure, I might have to return here," he said. "At least for part of the season. Liriano did before he got called up to Rochester. I'm willing to do that too. But if things get to the point where I don't see myself improving and am still inconsistent, I'd have to think seriously about quitting. I'd also talk to my agent and see what he thinks."

That was the first time Olson had mentioned having an agent. "I deal with Bob Lisanti," he explained. "He's with RMG Sports Management in Naperville, Illinois." At this point Justin explained that all his agent does is hook him up with the makers of gloves, bats, and shoes, and any other equipment he might need. "They get me that for free," he said. "Of course, if I get to be a free agent and need help signing a contract, he'll negotiate it. But you have to be with the organization for six years to become a free agent. By then I'd be 29." Clearly, Justin was not thinking that far ahead.

Before going inside to dress for practice, he admitted how surprised he was by the Rock Cats' sudden turnaround. "We're back in the race, but I still don't know quite how it happened," he said, ignoring the fact that Stan Cliburn attributed it partly to Olson's brilliant pitching performance against Bowie two weeks earlier—his 2-1 squeaker that started the streak.

"We struggled real hard at the beginning of the season," Olson continued. "Even though we played some great games, we couldn't seem to win. Maybe it takes a while for everything to jell."

He was right. The Rock Cats hitters were hot right now, and the starting pitchers, stingy in giving up hits and runs. With that combination it was obvious that the Rock Cats were going to win a lot of games. "Things are just kind of falling into place," Justin added. "We're playing the teams we need to beat to get into the play-offs, and we're beating them. The morale is great. And Stew and Stan are just loving it."

So was Bill Dowling. The general manager's ebullience was precipitated not only by the winning ball his team was playing, but by the cooperation he was getting from the Twins organization. "Minnesota sent us three of their number one prospects in the last two or three weeks," he beamed, glancing up at the TV mounted on his office wall.

Bill still liked to keep up with his former employer, the Yankees, who at that moment were engaged in a close game with the Twins. "How do you divide your loyalties," I asked, pointing to the screen.

"No problem," he said. "I'll always be a Yankee fan." But then he started telling me in glowing terms about the talent infusion recently given to the Rock Cats by the Twins. "Left-hander Glenn Perkins, a graduate of the University of Minnesota last year, was the Twins' number one draft pick," he explained. "He just came up from the Miracle along with shortstop Denard Span and third baseman Matt Moses. They not only give us more talent in those positions, they put pressure on the other players to compete in a significant way."

As a lawyer, Bill sometimes equates what goes on in a baseball stadium with what happens in a courtroom. "Being a trial lawyer," he explained, "I'd much rather try a case against a good lawyer than a lousy lawyer. You rise to the occasion. And I think our players, knowing how good these new prospects are, are also rising to the occasion. But that's only part of it.

"The other part is Stan Cliburn," Bill continued. "He has sort of a magical way of turning the team around during the second half of the season. He proved that both in 1991 and 1993. Let's hope it's the odd years. He's patient with these kids in April, May, and June, bringing them along to the point where he says, 'Listen guys, we're into the second half of the season, and we need to pick up the pace if we're going to make the play-offs.' It's the combination of Stan's philosophy and the new players."

Knowing Stan, I'm sure he used tougher words than those. But it was great hearing Bill sound so happy with his manager. "Just look at where we are," he added. "We've won nine games in a row and are only four games out of first place."

7

A SCOUT'S REPORT

I decided to stay in New Britain for a few more games while the Rock Cats were hot. The change in atmosphere from their May–June dry spell was striking. And now with the players' spirits so high, I wanted to soak up a little more of that euphoria for the book before going on to Rochester.

There was another reason for hanging around for the three-game home stand against Norwich. I'd been missing my daily chats with Stew. And I needed to catch up with him to find out his plans for Olson. There seemed to be some question about Justin's role since the arrival of two new pitchers: southpaw Glenn Perkins and right-hander Nick Blackburn. Where did that leave Justin? I wondered. Would he still be given spot starts?

I'd been unable to track down the pitching coach for an answer. He was either in a closed-door meeting or out throwing batting practice every time I dropped by his office. But coming out of the Super 8 Motel on the pristine, clear Friday morning of July 29, I found him in the parking lot confronted with a dead battery. Being a summer resident of Block Island where there is scant auto repair service, I always carry jumper cables in the back of my SUV. We soon had Stew's sporty red convertible humming, and then made a date to meet at the ballpark 15 minutes later.

No. He had no plans to keep Olson in the bull pen all the time. "He's made some good spot starts," Stew said. "He's a guy we need to pitch in doubleheaders and when the rotation guys miss a turn."

He then reminded me that Olson had already thrown more than 90 innings and had responded well to starting or coming out of the pen. "You know, I think he likes it out there. The guys get acclimated to the bull pen. They think it's their home."

Stew was obviously enjoying his team's winning streak. "The guys are feeding off each other," he claimed. "One guy gets a hit, and the next guy wants to get a hit, and it multiplies from there. Can you believe, we've gotten at least 10 hits in each of the last eight games? It's the same with the pitchers. One guy throws a good game, and the next guy wants to do the same thing. We're now in third place in our division, only four games out of a play-off spot. And we still have 31 games left to play. Two weeks ago nobody thought that would be possible. Not even the players themselves.

They're now so eager to win, they're showing up early for practice."

With the Rock Cats on a roll like that, going to the ballpark became addictive even for me. I looked forward to batting practice, chatting with the ushers, always full of gossip about the team, and with the reporters, who showed up early in the press box—sometimes, I figured, to get first licks at the free food.

Broadcaster Jeff Dooley, full of anecdotes and Rock Cats' lore, was usually the first to arrive. He, too, couldn't quite fathom the team's remarkable change of fortune. "You can tell," he said, "when the Cats are in contention. The players keep glancing at the scoreboard during a game to see if Portland and New Hampshire, the two league leaders, are losing."

By chance, in the course of covering the Rock Cats, I'd made friends with Lukas McKnight, a former catcher and presently a scout for the Chicago Cubs. His assignment was to evaluate and write reports on all of the Twins' minor-league players, including, of course, Olson and Liriano. Bald as a Buddha, and with his polished pate burned a deep tan from sitting in the sun behind so many home plates, he was easy to pick out even in a crowded ballpark. During the game against Norwich on July 30, I spotted him aiming his handheld radar gun at Olson who'd just been called in from the bull pen to stop a Navigator rally. I thought Justin had a pretty good night, allowing only two hits, one run, and no walks in three innings. His fastball looked sharp, and most importantly, he didn't groove any pitches that could be knocked out of the ballpark—his biggest weakness. But I wondered what the scout thought. His opinion obviously carried a lot more weight than mine.

Lukas seemed a little reluctant to say, but after we'd chatted a bit, he offered to send me his scouting reports on both Olson and Liriano. "I'll e-mail them to you," he promised.

By one of those remarkable coincidences, Lukas had been a catcher for Libertyville High in Illinois, and batted against Olson in the state finals. But it was only after I mentioned that Justin had gone to Oak Park High that he remembered him. "I can't believe it," he said. "Here I am scouting the same guy I tried to get a hit off."

As Lukas explained, his scouting reports rate each hurler's repertoire of different pitches: fastballs, breaking balls, sliders, and so on. "I put down two numbers separated by a slash," he said. "The first number is based on present performance, the second is my estimate of what that number might grow to in the future as the pitcher gains experience. In that way I am also rating the pitcher's potential. At least, that's how I do it," he added, implying that other scouts might use different systems. To these numerical scores he said he then adds a short but concise verbal report on the pitcher's strengths and weaknesses.

A few days later I received the following scouting reports on both Olson and Liriano:

OLSON, JUSTIN: right-handed pitcher.
Fastball: 57/57 (Slightly above major-league average).
Curveball: 50/50 (Major-league average or just average).
Changeup: 40/40 (Below average).

Control: 50/50 (Major-league average or just average).
Command: 40/45 (Fringe average).
Poise: 55/55 (Solid average).
Arm action: Long, from the time his hand leaves his glove until he releases the ball.
Delivery: High.

Strong chest and arms, strong lower half, but not bulky. Durable build. Athletic. Quick arm, but some effort in delivery. Not smooth. Arm action a bit long. Steps slightly open and shows ball, allows hitter to get a good look. Fastball is solid average, but flat and hittable. Throws strikes but command is not quite average. Curveball has good velocity but is not real sharp—not quite an out-pitch, but effective. Competes hard. Tries to create a run on changeup, but tips it off by slowing down arm. Hard worker.
One line summary: Organizational right-handed pitcher with solid average fastball, average curveball, hard worker.

LIRIANO, FRANCISCO: left-handed starter.
Fastball: 63/67 (Above average to well above average).
Change-up: 60/65 (Above average to well above average).
Slider: 65/70 (Well above average to very well above average).
Control: 55/60 (Solid average to above average).
Command: 40/45 (Below average to fringe average).
Poise: 40/50 (Below average to major-league average).
Arm action: Free. Very clean arm action that works very well.
Delivery: High

Built like Johan Santana, with wide shoulders and thin waist. Fastball overpowering at times, and gets good run to arm side. Can elevate fastball with good effect and gets swings and misses. Quick arm. Doesn't have great command of fastball, but fastball is good enough to get by without it. Power slider is an outpitch and overpowering at times. Slider has occasional depth, but breaks in hard on right-handed hitters. Gets good down-plane on everything, Likes to use changeup above average. Changeup has some run to arm side. Gets lots of swings and misses on changeup. Slows down arm occasionally on changeup. Maintains velocity late into games. Overthrows at times.

One line summary: Front line left-handed pitcher with power, fastball, slider, and above average changeup.

Liriano, as can be seen from the report above, scored considerably higher than Olson on his current ability. And being four years younger, with more time to develop, he also scored higher on future potential.

The reports were interesting, but so cryptic they struck me as crying for elaboration. "Can you interpret these reports for me?" I asked Lukas on the phone. "It would help to have a little more verbal description."

"That's the way I send them to the Cubs," he replied, taken aback by my apparent inability at deciphering his reports. But then as we chatted on, he patiently proceeded to tell me in more understandable terms what the various numbers revealed.

"When Olson releases the ball and comes down on his left leg," he explained, "it should not be off to the left so far that his legs are spread apart. It should be in a position pointing straight at the catcher, or even a little bit closed. That allows him to hide the ball better so the hitter doesn't see it until just a fraction of a second later." I wondered why the Cubs wouldn't insist on receiving their scouting reports in the very understandable form that Lukas was giving them to me over the phone. They were so much clearer and more descriptive that way.

"But when Justin steps forward with his left foot, he lands a little bit open," Lukas continued. "He's got a pretty good fastball, but the hitters get too much time to respond. They're able to catch up with the ball because they've had too long a look at it." That made sense. But why hadn't Stew mentioned the problem to me? I assumed he'd tried to correct it working with Olson out on the mound.

The scout had another criticism of Justin's delivery. "His arm circle from when he breaks with his glove to his release point, is too long."

"Do you carry a stopwatch and time the pitchers?" I asked naively.

Lukas laughed. "No, it doesn't necessarily take too long a time. What I mean is, there's too much of movement involved before he actually throws the ball. The most effective pitchers usually have very short arm action—very quick and to the point."

It amazed me how Lukas was able to detect these tiny flaws that I'm sure the fans never notice, or for that matter, the reporters who are supposedly experts.

I assumed from what Lukas just said, that he didn't have much hope for Olson moving up the minor-league ladder. But as it turned out that wasn't the case at all. "Actually, Olson wasn't pitching that bad," Lukas added. "Most of his pitches were pretty crisp. And as I recall he only gave up two hits and a run in the three innings."

Since this was a rare opportunity to get the scout's un-varnished opinion, I asked Lukas what he thought Olson's chances were of reaching the big leagues. "It all depends on how long he's willing to stick around and play," he explained. "Look at Aaron Small. Remember, just last month he was pitching for Trenton and beat the Rock Cats. Trenton was his 22nd professional team, most of them in the minors. Now he's starting for the Yankees and is helping to rescue their season. You know what? Olson's got better stuff than Aaron Small."

The scout then reminded me that Justin is still several years away from being a free agent. "If he's up there in Rochester in the next year or two and the Twins need a pitcher—maybe not a starter, but a reliever—he's got a pretty good chance of being called up."

Lukas finally got around to discussing Liriano. But his written report was so glowing, he didn't have much to add to it over the phone. "You see, Liriano's arm action is free," he said. "Kind of in-between long and short arm action. But in any case, it's very clean arm action and works very well."

Lukas then left no doubt that he expected to see the Dominican up in Minneapolis as soon as the major-league rosters are expanded. "Perhaps too soon," he indicated. "He's the only pitcher I've seen this season that will probably be a big-league star in a few years," he declared. "He's a young kid. He's going to have a long career, so there's no rush to get him up there. But my guess is the Twins won't want to wait and will call him up anyway."

After reading Lukas's reports and talking to him on the phone, I knew that in the future I'd be looking at both Olson and Liriano more critically, studying their windup, arm action, leg positions, and selection of pitches. The scout,

I realized, had given me a new perspective on all pitchers, not just the two of them.

Finally, I had to tear myself away from New Britain and go home to prepare for the extended trip to Rochester, Syracuse, and Pawtucket to see Liriano in action. The Dominican had already scored five wins against the lone defeat to Durham. And in the process he'd put up much better numbers than when he was pitching for the Rock Cats. "That's not unusual," Lukas told me. "Quite often the closer a pitcher comes to the majors, the more focused he is. I've seen that happen many times."

I was eager to see for myself how Liriano had progressed in the last five or six weeks. From everything I'd read and picked up on the Internet, he was fast becoming a star.

TWO BAD PITCHES

On August 5, my wife and I started off on the road to Rochester. We'd planned a leisurely drive through the Berkshires, perhaps with a stop to take in a concert at Tanglewood; then, on to Oneonta, New York, where I had served as a trustee at Hartwick College and where the Single-A Oneonta Tigers were celebrating the 100th anniversary of their antique stadium. Next we'd stop at the Baseball Hall of Fame in Cooperstown, and wrap up with a meandering back-roads drive through the wine vineyards of the Finger Lakes. But at the last minute, we scrapped most of those plans in favor of a detour through New Britain to attend the three-game, weekend series with Trenton.

Even though the Rock Cats had just returned from a

disappointing road trip, losing two out of three to Portland, the Trenton series was stirring up a lot of excitement. The Yankees had just sent center fielder Melky Cabrera and right-handed pitcher Calvin Maduro down from their Triple-A farm in Columbus to give the Thunder—as the visitors were called—a lift in their drive for a play-off spot. And as an added attraction for me, Olson, I discovered, was slated to start the final game of the series on Sunday, something I hadn't seen him do.

Justin never was able to disguise his boyish enthusiasm, so I could tell right away that he was pretty excited by the prospect of taking the mound against the number two team in the league. It also turned out that his wife, Jamie, his mother Dawn, and his grandparents were all flying in from Chicago to watch him pitch. So besides having a family reunion, he hoped to show them how well he was progressing in Double-A.

The Friday night game ended happily in a blowout for the Rock Cats. Behind 7 to 1 at the bottom of the sixth, they knocked out the highly rated Maduro and then tore through the Thunder's bull pen, scoring five runs in that inning and three more in the eighth to pull out a 9 to 7 victory. It also marked the 350th victory in five seasons for manager Stan Cliburn, who summed things up by proudly telling the local press: "The way we came back tonight can only build character. It was hustling baseball; it was fundamental baseball, and patient-at-bat baseball. It was a tribute to the guys who play the game hard." That was a lot more than the manager usually had to say publicly about his players.

On Saturday night, Olson showed up wearing shorts, a

T-shirt, and carrying a handheld radar gun and clipboard ready to chart the batters he would face the next afternoon. I asked if I could sit with him behind home plate. I knew that earlier in the season he'd started two games against the Thunder, and lost both. "You must be familiar with most of their hitters" is all I said, trying to be tactful and skirt mentioning the two defeats. "Yeah, and they beat me twice," he answered with his usual frankness.

There were some new faces in Trenton's lineup that Justin was wary of—especially slugger Melky Cabrera, one of the Yankees' hottest young prospects. "It's harder for me to get my slider in on left-handed batters like him," Olson admitted. And when the Trenton center fielder stepped into the batter's box and Olson watched him send the first pitch flying over the right-field fence, I understood his concern.

The game moved along swiftly with Jeff Karstens, Trenton's starter, blanking New Britain during the first six innings before he was pulled. At the same time his teammates ran up seven runs, just as they'd done the night before. But very quickly the Rock Cats' batters began teeing off on Trenton's relievers. For a few minutes it appeared that this game might turn into a repeat of Friday night's thrilling come-from-behind victory. Caught up in the excitement, Justin momentarily forgot his note taking and turned into a fan, cheering his teammates. But four runs were all the Rock Cats could muster this time, losing 7 to 4, and leaving Justin dejectedly clutching his clipboard full of markings, which looked like hieroglyphics to me.

Leaving the stadium, my wife and I ran into Olson and his family. His stunning blond wife, Jamie, was bubbling over with excitement. When I casually asked how she liked being married to a baseball player, it triggered a giggly little outburst, harking back to their senior year in high school.

"I noticed him first and went after him," she admitted unabashedly. "When he finally proposed, I liked the idea of being married to a baseball player, but I didn't know what I was getting into," she added, laughing and squeezing Justin's pitching arm. "Nobody in my family played baseball so I didn't really understand the game. You see, my older brother is a philosophy major and my younger brother is an art major," implying that those academic pursuits automatically excluded any interest in baseball. "I'm the middle sister, and this is all strange for me."

"Is there a problem being married to a baseball player?" I asked, hoping to provoke a few more of those spontaneously frank replies.

"Really, it's great," she smiled. "The only trouble is his pay is so low, I have to work and can't travel with him." Tomorrow, she explained, was one of the few times this season she'd be able to see her husband pitch. "Can't you see how thrilled I am?" she said.

Tomorrow's game was also going to be my last one in New Britain for a while. I planned to come back for a brief visit in late August. But between now and then all my time would be spent covering Liriano and the Red Wings. It occurred to me that I might not have the opportunity to see Olson pitch again, and I wanted to make the most of it, keeping track in my notebook of every pitch.

It was still an hour before game time when I spotted the sun glinting on the shiny bald head that could only belong to Lukas McKnight. I figured he must be finished scouting Olson. But Doug Deeds, the Rock Cats' leading hitter, who'd just recovered from a sprained leg, was back in the lineup. I thought it might be Deeds that the scout was following this time.

"Can I sit with you?" I asked, hoping he might give me a running critique of Olson's stint on the mound. The sun-drenched New Britain stadium was already more than half full, showing signs of a sellout. Lukas quickly removed his hat and radar gun from the seat next to him. "Actually, I'm taking another look at Olson," he explained.

There was no batting practice to watch in the morning after a night game, but the fans came early anyway, full of anticipation for a much-needed victory in the rubber game of this crucial series. "This one could be close," Lukas commented. "It'll be interesting to see how Olson takes the heat."

After the Rock Cats' nine-game winning streak ended in late July, the team had dropped to a position seven games under the 500 mark. So a lot was riding on Olson's strong right arm, especially on this day when he would not only be pitching in front of thousands of anonymous spectators, but with his wife, mother, and grandparents watching as well. I could imagine the pressure he was under. So I had skipped chatting with him down in the locker room before the game. "He doesn't fluster easily," I told Lukas. "But I've never seen him start a game before. This may be different."

Judging by the combined scores of the Friday and Saturday night games, the teams were evenly matched in hitting power. Trenton had scored a total of 14 runs, and New Britain, 13. But besides Melky Cabrera, Trenton's lineup contained several other powerful young sluggers that the Yankees were counting on for the future: first baseman Shelley Duncan, third baseman Eric Duncan (not related to Shelley), and designated hitter Mike Coleman, in particular.

With Lukas there, this was a wonderful opportunity for me to get a professional scout's view of how Olson attacked each of those tough batters. The scouting report he'd e-mailed me was a good appraisal of Olson's physical capability. But a running commentary on each pitch was something else. Hopefully, it would reveal some things about the right-hander's poise, strategy, and pitch selection as well.

The crowd, I decided, was too noisy to use my tape recorder, so I pulled out a large lined pad and planned to scribble notes as fast as Lukas relayed his thoughts. We watched in silence as Olson warmed up. He threw with easy, rhythmical motions belying much effort, although the pitch-speed gauge mounted on the right-field fence registered 92 and 93 mph.

Maybe it was because Olson's relatives were sitting directly behind us, eagerly waiting for the game to begin, that I, myself, felt the enormous weight of being out there on the mound in that situation. Yet, Justin looked calm and relaxed, popping one practice pitch after another into the mitt of catcher Gabby Torres. He's a cool, composed Rock Cat, I thought.

Without warning the game began and suddenly the balls and strikes were being counted. Olson quickly got two strikes on lead off batter Gabe Lopez, the second one lighting up the pitch-speed gauge with a super-fast 94.

"When he releases the ball, his stance is a little too open," Lukas whispered. "The hitter's getting too long a look at the ball. That way his fastball doesn't seem so fast to the batter." I remembered, that's exactly what he'd written in his scouting report.

The next pitch, a slider, was called a ball. "See," Lukas said, "after he releases the ball and comes down on his left foot, it slips off to one side of the mound. It should be right in front of the batter." Olson worked the count up to 3 and 2, before nicking the inside corner for a called third strike.

"He looks pretty sharp to me," I said, but Lukas didn't respond. The next batter, right-fielder Bronson Sardinha, also struck out. Jamie and Dawn and the grandparents must be thrilled, I thought. Justin's just mowing them down.

Now it was Melky Cabrera's turn at bat, the man Olson worried about when he was charting Trenton's hitters last night. Melky didn't leave any time for Lukas to comment. He swung at the first pitch and muscled a single over the shortstop's head.

"That open right foot of Olson's can also lead to shoulder problems," Lukas mentioned as Melky trotted to first.

That brought up cleanup hitter Shelley Duncan, the brawny first baseman the Yankees expect will someday replace Jason Giambi. Duncan led the Eastern League with 27 home runs, but that didn't seem to faze Olson, even though the gopher ball had been his nemesis.

Duncan swung and missed, twisting his body off balance, as the pitch-speed gauge registered another 94. Olson fired a second fastball. Duncan swung and missed again, this time lunging for a low-and-away ball way out of the zone. Then with the count 2 and 0, Justin grooved a fastball, this one right down the middle. Shelley swung and as Ken Lipshez reported in the next morning's *New Britain Herald*: "The ball may have reached all the way to the High School on the first bounce."

"After two strikes, he should have thrown a curveball," Lukas said. "And his fastball stayed belt high. A curveball would have gotten him back in rhythm."

I couldn't help but feel Justin's disappointment. He'd been so looking forward to proving to his family that professional baseball is a career worth pursuing even if the pay is poor. But he had no time to commiserate. The next batter, Eric Duncan, was a formidable hitter as well, and as Lukas pointed out, the number one prospect in the entire Yankees organization.

Olson still had his searing speed—and his confidence as well, it appeared. "His arm action's a little long," Lukas said, as Justin blew another 94 and then a 92 mph fastball right past Eric Duncan for strikes. "Too much time and movement from when his hand breaks with his glove to when he releases the ball," remarked the scout. I also remembered that same comment in his written report. Olson appeared to be committing all of the mistakes Lukas had previously detected.

Then as if Olson had heard Lukas's earlier comment about the need to regain his rhythm, he threw two looping curveballs that missed, sending the count to 2 and 2. Olson's speed was so impressive I felt sure he would now retire the side with another fastball. My prediction proved to be 50 percent correct. Olson fired another bullet. Eric Duncan swung hard, and like his namesake, sent the ball flying high over the fence—the 15th home run Olson had given up in less than 100 innings.

The author at New Britain Stadium in Connecticut. Photo by Helen Rowan.

Helen Rowan at New Britain Stadium. Author photo.

Justin Olson. Author photo.

Liriano relaxes following an outing with the Twins. Courtesy of the
Minnesota Twins.

Liriano pitching for the Twins. Courtesy of the Minnesota Twins.

It didn't really matter what happened after that. Olson struck out Mike Coleman, the last batter, and two more hitters before being replaced after the fourth inning with the score still 3 to 0.

"He's probably been using that open stance so long it comes naturally to him," Lukas explained. "But it makes his fastballs seem slower, and his curveballs more visible." Then as a scout whose business it is to scrutinize every detail of a player's performance, he added: "The success or failure of a pitcher is determined by little things like that."

Manager Stan Cliburn had another explanation for Olson's disastrous day on the mound. "It all goes to show it's not how hard you throw, it's location," he said. "We preach to our pitchers that when they're up two strikes and no balls, to change the eye-line and back the hitter off with something up in the zone. I don't know if Justin tried to get the ball up in the zone, but it went right down the middle."

Stan had told him. Stew had told him. And Olson knew himself that his own tremendous speed supplied half the power for all those home runs. Only half came from the batter's swing.

Trenton went on to win 4 to 2. Lukas charitably commented that Olson did better than the scoreboard indicated. "Most of his pitches were pretty crisp," he said, repeating that word he favored for cleanly and quickly released bullets. But Stan Cliburn, still miffed about Olson's poor choice of pitches, told reporters afterwards, "We lost that game in the first inning."

It was the first time I'd ever heard the manager pin the blame for a defeat on one player.

THE ROAD TO ROCHESTER

We had come to the ballpark with our bags packed for the first leg of the drive to Rochester. Fortunately for us, and I suppose for Olson too, the game ended early. That suited us fine since we hoped to see at least the last few innings of the night game in Oneonta, where the single-A Tigers were celebrating the 100th anniversary of their stadium. I'd been to a few games in that antique ballpark in 1991 when I was a trustee at Hartwick College. Oneonta was then a Yankee farm, starring pitcher Andy Pettitte and catcher Jorge Posada.

The game up there wasn't scheduled to start until 7 PM, plenty of time for us to make the trip without speeding or resorting to the thruways. We stuck to old Route 23, which winds through a series of picturesque towns in the southwest corner of Massachusetts—Monterey, Great Barrington, and Egremont—then crosses into New York State and over the Hudson via the Rip Van Winkle Bridge. Glancing back across the river, we could see perched high on the eastern bank, the ornate Persian-style castle called Olana, which was the last home of the celebrated nineteenth-century landscape painter, Frederic Church. Ahead, the road plunged deep into the Catskill Mountains and on to Oneonta, a once-important railroad hub nestled in the Susquehanna River Valley.

We stopped for a cup of coffee and a piece of pastry at a roadside bakery near Woodstock, still remembered the world around for its wild 1969 rock festival. We had only driven about 100 miles. But having sat in the sun for nine innings before that, I was already feeling drowsy and in need of some caffeine.

All the way I'd been thinking about Olson. Were those two momentous home runs going to kill his career? Were Stew and Stan finally going to give up on him as a spot starter, perhaps even as their middle-innings reliever? What could his family have thought, watching those two gopher balls sail over the fence? They'd been so excited the night before, anticipating a triumphant day on the mound for Justin. Then boom! boom! the game was over before it had really begun.

Those thoughts kept going through my head as we followed the twisting and turning road through the mountains. Well, at least Justin didn't lose his composure, striking out five of the first nine batters he faced, and blanking Trenton for the next three innings. That showed some courage, I thought.

The day before the game, I'd interviewed Rick Knapp, the minor-league pitching coordinator for the Twins. A large man with an iron-gray crew cut, his job was to keep tabs on all the pitchers from the Triple-A Rochester Red Wings down to the Rookie League Elizabethton Twins. I discovered in the course of our conversation that he had an interesting explanation for Olson's vulnerability to the home run ball.

"After all he's really a reliever," Rick said. "He comes into the middle of a game with that don't-give-up-a-hit, no-run mind-set. But starting, he's got more time to think about things. He may be trying to save himself, knowing he's going to pitch five or six more innings." That hadn't occurred to me. I regretted never having asked Olson if he found starting and relieving required different mind-sets.

"You know, if you try to finesse things too much," Rick added, "and start thinking about what you're going to pitch during the next couple of innings, you lose your concentration. Then, what do you know, the ball's flying out of the park."

It didn't look to me like Olson had been hoarding bullets for later in the game. Most of his pitches ranged from 90 to 94 mph while he racked up those five strikeouts. "I've reminded him," Rick said, "not to keep firing bullets one after another. 'Use your slider and changeup,' I told him. After all, he's worked on both of them pretty hard."

Rick also had some nice things to say about Olson. "He's done just about everything we've asked him to do: starting games, restoring order when the starter got roughed up, and coming in as a closer. He battled through some changes in his mechanics last year too, and his velocity's now back up again.

"You know," Rick added, as if I'd never met Olson and wasn't familiar with his background, "he sort of came out of nowhere from an independent league. But he's one of the nicest guys you'll ever meet, the all-American boy."

After those positive comments, I put the all-important question to Rick. "What do you think? Will Olson be returning here next year, or moving up to Rochester?"

"I just don't know how many guys will be moving up to the major-league level, or how many six-year free agents will be gone," he replied. "You have to figure on what I call the stair-step effect. Invariably, three or four guys get promoted from Fort Myers to New Britain. Then three or four make the jump to Rochester. If you have too many guys all deserving to jump one level higher at the same time, it plays havoc with all the teams."

He seemed reluctant to give me a straight answer about Olson's future. I'd already decided Justin would probably be stuck with the Rock Cats for a second season, when Rick ended the interview on a surprisingly optimistic note. "What we often do," he said, "is move a pitcher up for a couple of starts to see what he can do at the higher level. We give him a taste of it and then bring him back down if necessary." I was sure that would suit Olson just fine.

Jim Rantz, who outranked Rick, controlling the fate of all of the Twins' minor league players and not just the pitchers, had been somewhat ambivalent when I'd interviewed him about Olson's future. "One of our scouts picked him because of his arm strength," he explained. "He throws hard. He's got great size for a pitcher. He's got a good angle, and the ball comes out of his hand real nice. But he isn't consistent."

Then Rantz started chiding me for trying to pin him down on where Justin would be pitching next year. "The standard answer is, all our players are big league prospects," he said. "We give them plenty of attention, without pushing them, until they can compete at the next level. Anyway, the pitchers themselves pretty much let us know when they've hit high tide."

Rantz, I'd noticed, likes to remind people of what it was like for young pitchers back in his time. Or maybe he just veers off into a description of the old days when confronted with a question like mine that he doesn't want to answer.

"We didn't get all that special attention that pitchers do today," he said, instead of telling me where he thought Olson would be pitching next year. "They didn't ice our arms down after a game. The only ice we used was in our drinks. We didn't even have coaches. The manager was it— the pitching coach, batting coach, everything. And some of the ballparks we played in were nothing more than plowed-up potato fields."

But as I finally stood up to leave, Rantz added, smiling, "Yeah, I think Olson will get to the next level next year."

The game in Oneonta had already begun by the time we arrived. Dick Miller, the president of Hartwick College, drove us down to the ballpark and introduced Helen and me to the team's two venerable owners, Sam Nader, the city's 86-year-old former mayor, and 92-year-old Sid Levine. Dick had endeared himself to them by providing rooms for their players, and for the visiting team members as well, in the college dorms that were empty during the summer.

Sitting there, listening to Sam, as the Oneonta Tigers battled the Jamestown Jammers, I felt that we were back in the old bush-league era. The ancient cement grandstand, silhouetted by the lights, stood like a hundred-year-old ghost behind us. Just a sprinkling of fans remained sitting on its hard seats, most of them having slipped down to the more comfortable field boxes enclosed by blue iron railings, which Sam claimed were hand-me-downs from the Syracuse Sky-Chiefs. "They built a new stadium up there in 1996 and shipped us their old box seats," he said. "The batting cage is a hand-me-down, too," he added. "It was a gift from the Yankees in 1961."

The Oneonta stadium, now called Damaschke Field, he went on to explain, dates back to 1905 when it was called Elm Park after the beautiful old trees surrounding the diamond. "In those early days," he said, "the fans had the choice of paying to get in or watching the games for free from atop the Delaware & Hudson freight cars parked next door."

Coming into the ballpark I noticed that tickets cost $5 for adults and $4 for children. However, Sam explained that 16 of the 38 home games are sponsored by local businesses. "On those nights," he said, "no one has to pay."

I was surprised that the team is now a Detroit farm club, although I knew the Yankees had moved its Single-A, New York-Pennsylvania League franchise into the fancy new digs on Staten Island. "It doesn't matter where the players come from or what the team's called," Sam said handing me a copy of the ballpark's special 100th anniversary program. "When you read this you'll see that it's had many different names, starting with the Oneonta Red Lions."

The program described how on Memorial Day, 1905, the Red Lions opened the new stadium by taking on the Norwich Crescents. (The Crescents won 11 to 5.) "The grandstand was filled," the program stated, "and hundreds of men stood along both the first and third base lines." "You see," said Sam. "Baseball has been popular right from the beginning in this town."

As the Tigers scored a run and eked out a victory in the ninth inning, both owners stood up to cheer. I couldn't help but notice how spry they both seemed, even though they, like their stadium, were relics of a bygone baseball era. "We've owned this franchise for 41 years," announced Sam proudly. "And we hardly ever miss a home game."

We spent the night at Thornwood, the college president's official residence, where we'd stayed a few times when I was a trustee. It turned out that President Miller had grown up in Rochester and had been a member of the Red Wings' original Knothole gang (an organization that sold cheap tickets to kids, who in the old days watched games through knotholes in the outfield fence). But he'd never heard of Francisco Liriano and knew nothing about the team today. The only advice he gave us was to be sure to stop at the Corning Glass Museum on the way.

We would have preferred to meander along back roads to Corning. But to allow time to see some of the museum's incredible exhibits representing 3,500 years of glassmaking, and to eat lunch in the glass-enclosed cafeteria, we stuck to the superhighways. Even so, the wooded hills and open farmlands of upstate New York appeared beautifully peaceful and far removed from hectic New York City and its suburbs. Even Binghamton, a factory town spread over several of those hills, looked neat and clean and quiet—at least it did from Route 17 as we sped by.

When we arrived at Rochester's Crowne Plaza Hotel, the Ottawa Lynx players were also checking in. The Red Wings had booked us very conveniently where the visiting teams stay. I couldn't get over how big and brawny the Lynx players looked out of uniform, in their T-shirts and jeans. With broad chests, powerful shoulders, and bulging arm muscles, it took only three or four of them to fill an elevator, causing us some delay in getting upstairs.

Frontier Field, the home of the Red Wings, is handily situated in the center of the city, surrounded by the Eastman Kodak tower and other tall office buildings. It is just a 10-minute walk from the hotel to the stadium, so I decided to go pick up my press credentials even though August 8 was an off day for the Red Wings. I wanted to make sure I had them since Liriano was due to start pitching at 9:35 the next morning, a crazy hour, I thought, for a ball game. Another game was scheduled for that night. And Nick Blackburn, just promoted from the Rock Cats two days earlier, was scheduled to pitch that one. It was rumored that Liriano had been picked for the morning game because the sun would be behind him and in the batters' eyes, making it easier for him to pile up more strikeouts.

I could tell right away that the Red Wings take good care of the media. Walking into the empty stadium past a life-size horse made entirely of old baseball gloves, which stands in the main entrance, I was greeted by Chuck Hinkel, the team's public relations director. He had my temporary press pass, a Red Wings media guide, and several local articles about Liriano all ready for me. Glancing at the clippings, I noticed that the Dominican had now won six games. In the last one against league-leading Buffalo, he'd given up only one hit and one walk, while striking out thirteen in seven innings. "That," Chuck told me, "was Liriano's second one-hitter since coming to the Red Wings."

I walked around the cavernous concourse filled with unmanned and unlit food and beverage stands, trying to familiarize myself with the modern 10,840-seat ballpark. I discovered that it also had grassy berms out in right and left field that could accommodate another thousand or so picnickers, and a hot tub in center field that could be rented by partiers for $125 a game. Imagine sitting with your friends sipping beer in the hot bubbling water while the ballgame is going on. I must have spent an hour on my explorations. The Kodak tower was already lighted when I left the stadium.

That night the daughter of a friend of ours and her husband took us to a popular barbeque restaurant called the Dinosaur. Located in the heart of town and looking very rundown, it sits beside the Genesee River that also looked rundown, having been reduced to a trickle during the summer drought. About a hundred Harley Davidson motorcycles were parked outside.

"This place is patronized mainly by bikers," our host mentioned, as if that wasn't perfectly obvious, and became even more obvious after we walked inside and discovered that we were about the only untattooed patrons.

"You might find a few ball players, too," our host mentioned, though Liriano was the only member of the Red Wings I would have been able to recognize. And surely, he wouldn't hang out in a place like this, since I was told he didn't drink beer or party, or for that matter, do anything much besides throw baseballs.

A bar with some two dozen polished brass taps for draft beer occupied kind of a no-man's-land between several packed dining rooms suffused with the tantalizing aroma of sizzling barbequed ribs, sausage, and chicken. We were given a number and told to take our beers outside and wait where all the Harleys were parked, though in a matter of minutes we heard our numbers called over the PA system.

My plan, I mentioned to our friends, was to attend the three home games, including the morning-night doubleheader the next day against Ottawa, then drive to Syracuse for the two games there against the SkyChiefs, finally returning to Rochester for four more games against the PawSox. That schedule would allow me to see Liriano pitch twice, besides providing considerable time to interview him in the clubhouse or when he was resting in the dugout.

For Helen, that seemed like an awful lot of unrelieved baseball. She could sketch the two ballparks. But then what? Our host's wife came to her rescue. It turned out that she worked for the George Eastman House and its International Museum of Photography and Film.

"While Roy's covering the ball game tomorrow morning," she offered, "I'll show you around the museum and the magnificent Italian-style gardens surrounding Eastman's former residence." That was just fine with Helen, an avid gardener, who'd also worked as a picture editor for *Life* magazine before we were married and had retained an interest in photography. It also turned out that our hosts were Red Wings fans. In return I offered to get tickets for the game Blackburn was pitching in the evening, so all of us could go.

10

THEY CALL HIM
THE "ZERO HERO"

By 8:30 the next morning, an hour before Liriano was slated to take the mound against the Ottawa Lynx, I was already poking around Frontier Field looking for people in the front office to talk to. I had called General Manager Dan Mason from New Britain and even though we didn't make a specific appointment, he spotted me wandering around, looking lost, I presumed. In any case, he immediately escorted me into his office. His trim athletic build, neatly clad in coat and tie, made me think, "This is the real-life Dapper Dan."

"I guess you're following Liriano," he said, although on the phone I'd told him only that my mission was to gather information for a book about minor-league baseball. In any case, he welcomed me warmly. "Everybody's interested in Francisco," he said. "He's causing quite a stir. The reporters here call him the 'Zero Hero' because of all his shutouts."

Without my even asking, Dan continued talking about his recently acquired star. "Unfortunately, I didn't make spring training this year," he said, "but I'd heard a lot about Liriano from Phil Roof, our manager." I knew that Roof's wife was very ill and that the Twins had turned the managerial reigns over to hitting coach Rich Miller. So I mentioned to Dan right then that Rich was high on my list of people I wanted to interview about the Dominican lefty.

"Liriano's a special talent. No doubt about it," Dan continued. "And he's a pretty good draw for us, generating excitement among our fans who want to see him pitch before he moves up to Minnesota."

"Is that a given?" I asked. But Dan didn't answer, veering off instead into description of the close relationship between the Twins and Red Wings. "Jim Rantz does such a good job of keeping us in the loop," he explained. "And when the fans see a player at Frontier Field one week, and on ESPN the following week playing for Minnesota, they feel like they know him. That's why right now they can't get enough of Liriano. They're fascinated by the way he'll throw 97 one minute and 82 the next, striking out one batter after another."

But Dan worried a bit about how quickly the young Dominican was being built into a superstar by the media. "It's putting tremendous pressure on him. Still, when he's out there on the mound he shows a lot of calm and never seems rattled. That says something about a kid who's only 21."

Even though the game was due to start in 15 minutes, the general manager seemed eager to keep on chatting. So I asked how he broke into the baseball business. "I was in the Knothole gang," he said, "a big fan of the Red Wings when I was a kid. After graduating from Notre Dame I began working for the team, first as an intern, then as group sales director. When Joe Altobelli became GM, he asked me to be his assistant."

Dan could see that the name didn't register with me, although I'd noticed "Altobelli's Delli" among the concessions in the food court under the grandstand. "He's done everything," Dan explained. "He was a player here in the mid-sixties, our manager from '71 through '76, then manager of the San Francisco Giants, coach for the Yankees and Cubs, before becoming manager of the Orioles when they won the 1983 World Series. After that he came back here as GM from '92 to '94. Working under Joe was the turning point in my career."

Since Dan is a hired hand and not an owner as Bill Dowling is, I wondered what his responsibilities are. "My job is managing the business side: tickets, promotions, advertising," he replied. "The bottom line is to see that the fans have a great time. You could say I'm the director of fun."

Returning the conversation to Liriano, I asked if he was surprised to get the young lefty so early in the season, especially since his record with the Rock Cats wasn't outstanding. "No," he replied, "Liriano was one of the names we hoped to see. There was a lot of anticipation about him. So far he's exceeded our expectations."

By the time Francisco uncorked his fastball for a strike on lead off batter Bernie Castro, the stadium was more than two-thirds full, quite surprising for a Monday morning. Public relations director Chuck Hinkel announced to reporters in the press box that the crowd included 1,700 "walk-up" ticket-buyers that morning, testifying to Liriano's personal drawing power.

The Lynx, I learned, were the second best hitting team in the International League, boasting an array of dangerous hitters including Walter Young, Napoleon Calzado, and Bobby Darula. Liriano, with a string of 19 consecutive scoreless innings to protect, had studied them carefully during the two weekend games up in Ottawa, where the Lynx batters buried Rochester under a barrage of 31 hits and 23 runs. The face-off just beginning between the Lynx sluggers and the Dominican strikeout specialist reminded me of that question kids used to ask: What happens when an unstoppable force meets an immovable object?

As it turned out, the Lynx weren't unstoppable, and Liriano was still immovable, extending his scoreless innings to 26 and lowering his ERA to 1.46.

As soon as it was over, I followed Chuck Hinkel and a trailing crew of reporters and photographers down to the clubhouse in the basement. I was curious to see if Liriano would show any more animation after his seventh Red Wings' victory than he did on the day he bid the Rock Cats good-bye.

His tan, lithe body was clad only in shorts. And as the

Rochester Democrat and Chronicle reported, "He was wearing an ice pack on his left shoulder and a smile on his face." I was happy to see that he recognized me, since my time with him in New Britain had been so short. "Everything feels real good," he said nodding in my direction. "My pitches are working good. And the guys are making plays behind me."

Three short sentences strung together. That's a record for Liriano, I thought—at least in English. Like the other Hispanic players babbling away behind him, I suspected he might have said more in Spanish. Then groping for one final remark before returning to his locker to get dressed, he added, "That was fun."

Surely, it wasn't all fun. Twice he verged on serious trouble. In the fifth inning he temporarily lost his concentration and walked the first two batters. In the sixth he had men on first and third, before throwing three straight strikes to end the inning.

Outside the stadium where he stopped to sign autographs for a knot of clamoring kids, I heard a few fans voicing disappointment with his showing. "Hey, Liriano, how come you let 'em have four hits?" shouted an old geezer hobbling away on a cane. I suppose that was understandable, since he'd thrown back-to-back one-hitters against Charlotte on July 29 and Buffalo on August 4. Nevertheless he'd held the Lynx scoreless for seven innings. The fans are becoming unreasonable, I thought. They expect too much from their Zero Hero.

I was more surprised later that afternoon, when I returned to the clubhouse to interview pitching coach Bobby Cuellar and heard him also voice displeasure with Liriano's performance. "Today was his worst start since he's been here," Bobby said. "He reached out too far and muscled too much. Didn't you see? He locked himself up during his windup and jerked too hard. I had to go out to the mound a couple of times and calm him down."

Born in Alice, Texas, not far from the Mexican border, Bobby is fluent in Spanish. For that reason he'd developed a much closer relationship with the Dominican than Stew Cliburn had. "I first met Francisco during spring training at Fort Myers," Bobby explained, a hint of a Spanish accent creeping into his squeaky, high-pitched voice. "I thought he was going to be pretty good. But he was very young, and he had a few things to learn. I tried to help him a bit before he went off to New Britain."

Bobby claimed to be a great believer in physical fitness. "The pitcher needs to know a lot about his body so he can correct things when they're going wrong. Sometimes, Frankie," he said using the nickname the Red Wings players gave Liriano, "gets a little out of control and he tries to throw harder and work faster than he should. Usually that's not the way to do things. Veteran pitchers don't throw harder. They just kind of lay back and slow down a bit."

It was obvious the pitching coach felt genuine affection for his protégé. "He's got a good arm, but he's also blessed with a good attitude and good aptitude," Bobby added. "He listens, and he's quick to learn.

"Before he came here," Bobby continued, "he had shoulder and elbow problems, though not much this year. I've tried to change things so he doesn't put so much strain on his arm. I've really focused on trying to get him a bit of leverage so he can finish his motion nice and easy and free. He's been working on that for the last five or six starts and I thought he'd gotten pretty good at it. But then today, he was a little bit off." If Liriano was off today, I wondered how he'd do when he was on.

"What's his future?" I finally asked, expecting to elicit nothing but praise. "It's not my job to put labels on people," he replied, and then launched into a comparison between Liriano and Johan Santana. "Santana was here when he also was 21. We had to work on his mechanics. We had to cut his motion down. They both have overpowering fastballs, the one thing that's hard to teach. I don't think Santana's faster. Santana has an exceptional changeup. This kid has a pretty good changeup. Santana's sliders are good. So are Liriano's." I got the impression that Bobby believed Liriano would probably prove in the future to be the equal of the Cy Young Award winner.

Bobby also claimed that Liriano, himself, was disappointed in the way he'd pitched this morning, although he certainly didn't show it down in the clubhouse after the game. "If you've been around young players long enough, you know they're sky-high when things are going well and down in the dumps when they aren't." Of course, I'd never seen Liriano show enough animation to know if he felt high or low. In fact, none of the other press people covering him thought he had much of a personality. "He acts like he's in neutral," I remembered Ken Lipshez, the *New Britain Herald* reporter, once saying.

The night game turned out to be an 11-inning marathon that didn't fill my wife with joy. Looking down from the press box, I could see her shifting restlessly in her seat beside our two friends. Right-hander Nick Blackburn, in his Triple-A debut, wasn't spectacular, but pitched six solid innings, allowing three runs on eight hits. The score was tied in the third inning. Ottawa went ahead in the fifth before Rochester tied it up again in the eighth, in what was becoming a nail-biter for everyone there except my wife.

As the teams headed into the 11th inning with no sign that the game was going to end there, *Democrat and Chronicle* reporter Jim Mandelaro mentioned that Rochester held the record for the longest game of professional baseball ever played. "It's an amazing story," he said, "and I'm reminded of it every time a game goes into extra innings."

Jim then described how at exactly 4:07 on Easter morning in 1981, in a contest against the PawSox in Pawtucket, umpire Jack Lietz, under orders from the International League president, suspended the game before the start of the 33rd inning with the score tied at two. (Boy, wouldn't my wife have loved that one, I thought.)

Sixty-five days later on June 23, play was resumed in Pawtucket before a crowd of 5,756 fans, with millions more listening in on the Armed Forces Radio Network. The 33rd and final inning took only 18 minutes. Dave Kozas hit a single with the bases loaded, and the PawSox won 3-2.

"Nobody felt worse than losing pitcher Steve Grilli," Jim Mandelaro said. "He'd been with the Toronto Blue Jays when the first 32 innings were played. But he'd been released and signed as a free agent with Rochester. Grilli started the 33rd inning and promptly loaded the bases before

Dave Speck came in and gave up the decisive hit. But it was Grilli who was charged with the loss.

"If you stop by Cooperstown on your way home," Mandelaro suggested, "you'll find Grilli's cap on display at the Baseball Hall of Fame."

Fortunately for my wife and the other 5,630 fans at Frontier Field who were anxious to go home and go to bed, nothing even approaching that incredible game in Pawtucket was about to reoccur. With the score tied at five in the bottom of the eleventh, Luis Rivas doubled and went to third on Jason Tyner's sacrifice bunt. Then Luis Maza hit the first pitch into the left-field bull pen, giving Rochester a 7 to 4 victory and a sweep of the two games that day that couldn't really qualify as a doubleheader because they required separate tickets. The back-to-back wins, however, put the Red Wings nine games over the 500-mark and only half-a-game behind first-place Buffalo.

During the game I'd been fortunate to sit next to Joe Altobelli, the former first-baseman-coach-manager-cum-everything-including-Hall-of-Famer that Dan Mason called his mentor. Joe, or "Alto" as everybody in the press box called him, handled the between-innings-color for WHTK-AM Radio. But apparently after broadcasting the morning game, he was enjoying a night off. His slightly stooped, big-boned frame barely fit in the chair, and I could see how a baseball bat would have looked like the proverbial toothpick in his monster hands. If anybody could, I figured he'd be able to give me an honest evaluation of the young Dominican's potential.

Right away Alto admitted how impressed he was with Liriano's maturity. "He reminds me of Dennis Martinez," he said. The former manager then explained that Martinez pitched for the Red Wings in 1976 and was the last player in the International League to win the triple-crown: most wins, most strikeouts, and lowest ERA. Dennis, he also reported, went on to win 245 games for the Expos, Braves, and Mariners. "I expect Liriano will have the same success in the big leagues," Alto predicted.

Our friends escorted my wife back to the Crowne Plaza after the game. But I was on a roll, collecting different opinions of Liriano, and wanted to stay on to interview Rich Miller, the Red Wings' acting manager. Rich had played center field for the Mets' farm teams in the seventies, getting up as far as Tidewater in Triple-A. "My minor-league batting average was 256," he said. "If it had been a little higher, I probably would've made the majors."

Rich, unlike his pitching coach, was full of praise for Liriano's showing that morning. "After all, he had to get up and pitch a 9:30 AM game after riding the bus back from Ottawa all day yesterday," Rich noted. "But he seems able to pitch at any hour or in any kind of weather. In Charlotte he started a 12:15 PM game when the temperature was 109 degrees. You probably want the Latin pitchers on the real hot days," he added as an afterthought.

The manager, of course, hadn't watched the Dominican battle the cold, to which the Rock Cats' trainer had attributed his poor early-season numbers. "One of our biggest concerns," Rich added, "is that he'll go home and play winter ball in the Dominican Republic. That would be foolish since he had shoulder and elbow problems a couple of years ago."

I finally put the question to Rich that I'd been asking everybody else in the Red Wings' organization. "Will the Twins call him up this season?"

"There are many factors involved," he answered, trying, I thought, not to convey the impression that the Dominican was about to be plucked suddenly from the Red Wings as he had been from the Rock Cats. "If the Twins are in the play-offs, they might want him. But if they feel we have a chance to make the play-offs, I think they'll leave him here. Every coach will tell you, watch a pitcher in a play-off drive when the chips are down, and you'll get a much clearer picture of his ability. The good guys really shine."

There was no question that the acting manager was aiming for at least a wild-card spot in the play-offs and was counting on Liriano to help him get there.

11

APPOINTMENT IN SYRACUSE

Having been unsuccessful in arranging any time alone with Liriano, I started dogging Chuck Hinkel to set something up for me during the Red Wings' two-game series against the SkyChiefs in Syracuse on August 11 and 12. It seemed like the perfect time to strike. Francisco wasn't scheduled to pitch either night and would be just exercising or perhaps throwing warm-up pitches to Bobby Cuellar before batting practice.

I had complete confidence in Chuck. A warm and high-spirited PR man, he liked to say: "I grew up in the ballpark." He started working for the Red Wings 15 years ago when he was only 19. After all that time he'd developed a very good relationship with the managers, coaches, and players and knew just when to collar them for interviews and when to leave them alone. He never cajoled, never insisted, even though Liriano and the other young players knew that dealing with the media was part of their job. Jim Rantz had made a point of that from the time they joined the Twins' organization. So I counted on Chuck to corral Liriano for what I hoped would be a heart-to-heart talk about his career and family.

Still, knowing how uncommunicative the Dominican is, Chuck couldn't promise anything. But assuming things would work out, my wife and I packed up and took off on the 100-mile straight-shot drive due east on U.S. 90 for Syracuse. If you've never traveled that stretch of highway, mind my word, it's a boring, six-lane strip of concrete that you might conclude was not a road for travelers, but a Nascar racetrack. We seemed to be the only car moving slower than one of Liriano's 97-mile-an-hour bullets.

We decided to save the longer, more picturesque drive, passing by the tips of the Finger Lakes on routes 5 and 20, for the return trip to Rochester, where Liriano was due to pitch again on Sunday, August 14. Chuck loved it when Liriano's turn in the rotation fell on a weekend, because with a little extra publicity the Red Wings could count on drawing a huge crowd.

We checked in at the Ramada Inn on Buckley Road on the scrubby western outskirts of Syracuse. Nothing much there except for a crossroads with a couple of gas stations, a Dunkin' Donuts, and a fruit-and-vegetable stand. The motel's only attraction, I decided, was its proximity to Alliance

Bank Stadium, home of the SkyChiefs. The Red Wings were also booked at the Ramada, and I figured even if Chuck failed me, I might be able to corner the Dominican in the dining room during breakfast. I know better now. The players don't seem to eat breakfast after a night game. Or maybe it's because their food allowance on the road is so skimpy they can't afford to. In any case I never saw one of them in the dining room day or night.

At the ballpark it became clear that besides Chuck, I had to deal with Andy Gee, the SkyChiefs public relations director, for any assistance required. A determined young man, he wanted to make sure that despite my interest in Liriano, I didn't entirely neglect his team. He promptly turned me over to Ron Gersbacher, the "Team Historian," whom I suspect is one of the few people in minor-league baseball to hold that high-sounding title. Ron in turn wanted to make sure that I knew the highlights of the SkyChiefs' history and filled me with a slew of interesting trivia that I duly jotted down in my notebook:

The first organized baseball game in Syracuse in 1858 pitted the local married men against the bachelors. The marrieds won 31 to 30, although in the return game the bachelors prevailed 37 to 24. In 1876 the first "curved pitch," or breaking ball as it is known today, was thrown by Syracuse ace Patrick Henry "Harry" McCormick. In 1879 Syracuse joined the National League, but did not finish the season because of financial problems. In 1910 the mighty Grover Cleveland Alexander won 29 games for the Syracuse Stars, concluding the season by hurling 52 scoreless innings. And so it went, right up to 1934 when Syracuse became the Chiefs. (When the team took flight and added "Sky" to its name, Ron didn't say.)

I was still waiting to hear from Chuck about when my session with Liriano might take place. My wife and I sat through the first game of the series in which the Red Wings got bombed 10 to 5. We enjoyed our new surroundings, nevertheless. As the farm team of the Toronto Blue Jays, the SkyChiefs occupied a newer and fancier double-decked stadium than the Red Wings' Frontier Field, providing a fresh sketching challenge for my wife. However, we were accustomed to seeing baseball played on grass, and it was difficult adjusting to the teal-blue Astroturf. They could have at least dyed the carpet a lush green, I thought.

The game turned out to be quite exciting. As we only learned the next morning from the *Post-Standard*, the Sky-Chiefs' first baseman Kevin Barker had arrived at the stadium with a throbbing migraine headache. "I never considered sitting out the game," he announced manfully, "because we're in the hunt for a play-off spot, and I'm going to go out there and help the team any way I can." He was also determined to help atone for his team's humiliating loss the previous night to last-place Scranton/Wilkes-Barre. Syracuse had been leading in that game 2 to 0 in the sixth inning but ended up being whipped 12 to 2.

The contest with Rochester was tied at 3 going into the bottom of the fourth inning. Barker had already hit a double in the first inning. Coming to bat again with the bases loaded in the fourth, he proved to be as the *Post-Standard* also reported, "a major headache for the Red Wings," by sending the first pitch sailing over the right-field wall for a grand slam.

Finally, the next afternoon Chuck called with word that I should be in the visitors' dugout at 2 PM. "Batting practice won't have started yet," he said, "and you and Liriano can chat quietly." That sounded very encouraging, but I still wondered if the elusive left-hander would show up, especially if Chuck didn't plan to deliver him personally.

I arrived 10 minutes early, and to my surprise Liriano was already sitting there, staring out at the empty stadium and swinging his left arm in circles to loosen it up. He was dressed in a T-shirt, jeans, and sneakers, it being too early to suit up for the calisthenics and other warm-up drills before batting practice. I thought I detected a slight welcoming smile cross his lips when he saw me coming, tape recorder in hand. Still, the challenge, I knew, was going to get him to answer my questions with more than just a "yes" or "no." Otherwise, my tape was going to consist mainly of my own questions, an occurrence that may not be so noticeable during the interview, but is extremely aggravating when you hear it played back.

"How are you feeling?" I asked, since Bobby Cuellar had mentioned that these young players are usually up sky-high or down in the dumps. Anyway, it was a harmless enough question to get the conversation rolling.

"I feel good," he answered, repeating the same three words he said after pitching the seven scoreless innings against Ottawa. "How about your left elbow?" I asked. "Is it giving you any trouble?"

"No," he replied. "This year I've worked hard to stay

119

healthy. Things have gotten better and better. Bobby's been helping me," he added. "He showed me some things I was doing wrong."

That was the most complete answer I'd ever heard Liriano give. And as the interview proceeded, he seemed to become even more relaxed and talkative. Maybe it takes as much time for him to loosen up during a conversation, I thought, as it does for him to warm up on the mound.

"I listen to Bobby and I try to get better every time I pitch," he continued. It didn't occur to me after my own conversation with the Red Wing's pitching coach, how dependent on him the young Dominican had apparently become.

He went on to explain that it was Bobby who taught him how to throw with an easier arm motion, how to keep his whole body more relaxed between pitches, and not to rely only on his fastball when he got in trouble. He sounded very grateful for Bobby's counsel.

"How about the batters up here in Triple-A?" I asked. "Are they a lot tougher than the ones you faced in New Britain?"

"They may be a little tougher. They don't strike at so many bad balls. But Bobby tells me to be myself. Just pitch to the mitt and don't worry about what the batters do."

Since the pitching coach had already enumerated the things Liriano had been doing wrong when he arrived in Rochester, I didn't pursue that line of questioning any further. Changing the subject, I asked about his family. All I knew was that they lived in San Cristobal, a sugar refining town just east of Santo Domingo, the capital of the little Caribbean country whose main industry seemed to be turning out top-quality baseball players for the major leagues.

"There are 10 children in my family," he said, actually volunteering this information. "Seven boys and three girls. I'm the youngest. My oldest brother is 38."

"Do you talk to your family very often?" I asked, wondering how hard it was to reach San Cristobal by phone. Through the Internet I'd found that it was the birthplace of the former Dominican dictator, Rafael Trujillo, and that Trujillo had built his palace there. So presumably a workable phone system must have been established, if for no other reason than to service Trujillo's calls.

"Yes, I talk to them every day," he said. With that opening, I asked if he'd mind giving me their number, as I planned to have a Spanish-speaking reporter friend in Puerto Rico call and interview them. I suspected he might want to protect his parents from the kind of grilling he was getting from me. But, no, he offered the number willingly.

"Since you and your father are both named Francisco, what does your family call you?" I asked.

"My parents and brothers and sisters all call me 'Kelben,'" he answered without any coaxing, though I suspected it might have been an embarrassingly cute nickname. "I don't know what it means," he claimed. "It's just what they call me." I also sensed from the note of sadness creeping into his voice, that the mention of his nickname might have made him homesick.

"How about your brothers, do any of them play baseball?" I asked, wondering if there was another pitcher in the Liriano family pipeline that we might soon be hearing about.

"No," he answered. "Nobody else in my family plays baseball," he said, though that hardly seemed possible in a country where practically all life revolved around the game. "I'm the only one."

"Was your father once a baseball player?" I asked.

"Sometimes my father and I played catch together but he was not a baseball player. We had a farm and he used to have many cows to take care of. But now he doesn't have the farm anymore."

Later, from my Spanish-speaking reporter friend who interviewed the father, I learned that the "many cows" were actually just eight, and that he now runs a *Colmado*, a tiny neighborhood store that sells a little of everything including lottery tickets. But his father could end up a rich man, I thought, if his son is called up by the Twins.

The father also revealed to my Spanish-speaking friend that Liriano has a 14-year-old half-brother, Francisco Xavier, whom he claimed may turn out to be an even better baseball player than the Red Wings' ace. "He runs and throws very well," the father said.

"When did you start playing baseball?" I asked, trying to switch the conversation back to the left-hander's career.

"I always dreamed of being a baseball player, even when I was only 10 or 11," he said. "Sammy Sosa was my hero then. I didn't plan to be a pitcher. I wanted to become a great home run hitter like him."

Sosa, I knew, was also a Dominican. But I was trying to calculate how old he would have been when Liriano was 10. In any case the conversation was now flowing pretty well.

"When I was 10 I played in a little league," he continued. "Not like the Little Leagues up here. They were just sort of pickup teams. I never went to any of the baseball academies the big leagues have in Santo Domingo. But I started playing professionally there when I was 16. I was a good hitter and played the outfield. But I was a slow runner. That's where the San Francisco Giants saw me play and signed me to a contract."

"Did they give you a bonus?" I asked.

"Yes," he said grinning, but he wouldn't tell me how much. I assumed that meant that it was very small.

"Were you happy with the Giants?" I knew he'd pitched for three or four of their farm teams before being traded to the Twins. "Yes, I liked the Giants' organization," he replied. "But you always have to be ready to be traded."

"And speaking of being traded," I said, "there were rumors floating around a few weeks ago that the Twins wanted a new second baseman and went after Alfonso Soriano. But the only player the Texas Rangers would accept in return was you."

"I don't know anything about that," he said, smiling. "I heard the rumors, too, but nobody talked to me about it."

I told him that I wanted to keep talking to him during the rest of the season. "I'm going to see you pitch back in Rochester, and then again in Pawtucket. But maybe we could also chat on the phone sometimes when you aren't charting opposing batters or pitching." That was agreeable with him and he gave me his cell-phone number.

There was just one more question I wanted to ask. "A

number of reporters claim you remind them of Johan Santana," I said, knowing that the Twins' ace had long since replaced Sammy Sosa as Liriano's idol.

"I met him during spring training," he replied. "Bobby introduced me to him. Johan watched me pitch and then he told me some things. He said I was young and should not throw so hard all the time. 'Take your time. Relax. You are going to be pitching for many years,' he said. He was very nice."

I was sure that must have been an inspirational encounter for Liriano. I could tell from the way his dark brown eyes shone when he mentioned the Cy Young Award–winner's name.

"What are you going to do this winter?" I asked, knowing that Jim Rantz was against his pitching winter ball and risking another arm injury. "I want to pitch in my country," he replied, a little tentatively. "My family's never seen me pitch. But I don't know how many innings the Twins will let me pitch." Rantz had already told me they might have to relent and let him throw 15 or 20 innings, but no more.

"Well," I said, "before you know it, you'll be back up for spring training. Maybe you should just rest when you're home."

I got the feeling he didn't like the idea at all of just resting during the off-season. Pitching and playing baseball were too much in his blood. In fact, I wondered if he ever thought about anything else. "If I can't play baseball, I'm not happy," he admitted.

From our conversation I wasn't sure if Liriano realized that I'd been following him all the way from spring training down in Fort Myers or that I was writing a book that was focused to a great extent on him. Our previous encounters had been too brief for me to do more than pop a few quick questions. Yet I decided there was no point now in confusing things by explaining that I was also covering his former teammate and friend, Justin Olson, and using the two of them as the central characters in a story about chasing the dream to become big-leaguers. All I said was, "You know, I've been watching you pitch ever since spring training."

"You saw me pitch against the Red Sox?" he said quizzically, suggesting that he found it hard to believe that any sane reporter would go all the way down to Florida to watch him throw a few innings.

"Yeah," he added, sheepishly. "Did you see David Ortiz hit that grand slam off me?"

12

BAD DAY AT FRONTIER FIELD

On the return trip to Rochester, we stopped for lunch at Port Byron, a quaint town on an offshoot of the old Erie Canal. Several small cafés fronted the concrete quay. We picked one where we could look out at the pleasure boats passing through the locks on their way to and from Lake Owasco.

We had stayed up late watching the Red Wings suffer another defeat by the SkyChiefs. A cloudburst with a fireworks display thrown in kept us there for an extra hour-and-a-half, so I decided to skip the game against Pawtucket in Rochester tonight and turn our trip back from Syracuse into a scenic tour. Besides, the wide-ranging interview with the reclusive Liriano made me more confident about the way the book was progressing. At last he seemed ready to cooperate without my having to use Chuck Hinkel as a foil.

From Port Byron we proceeded leisurely past Cayuga Lake, where several brides and grooms were posing en masse for a wedding picture by the shore, then on through Seneca Lake State Park and into the town of Canandaigua. We stopped at a combination bakery and café for coffee. One of the regulars confessed to being a collector of old *Life* magazines and claimed to be familiar with my byline, an occurrence that always amazes me since the weekly folded in 1972. From there we turned north onto the expressways funneling into Rochester.

Having a day off from baseball, I must admit, felt great. For most fans, I realized, going to a game is an infrequent and enjoyable outing. But I was beginning to see how for the players who spend almost every summer night or day at the ballpark, a feeling of drudgery could creep into the sport. In any case, I didn't feel guilty skipping a night. Liriano would be charting the Pawtucket batters for his turn on the mound the next day so there wouldn't be any chance to chat with him.

Come Sunday morning a low overcast blanketed Rochester. But that didn't deter the fans from pouring into Frontier Field early for the 1:35 PM game. Almost all the seats were filled by the time the overcast turned into a slow drizzle, dampening the field, but not the spirits of the crowd. Umbrellas blossomed and the tarps were rolled out as the two teams disappeared back into their dugouts. When the drizzle became a downpour, the game was cancelled, much to the displeasure of those prepared to sit out the storm. With a roar they booed the announcement.

I'd already come to realize just how hard core those local fans are. Baseball is deeply rooted in Rochester. In fact, many residents believe the game actually originated there in 1825, played in a meadow bordering the Genesee River. According to Thurlow Weed, a local printer at the time, "A baseball club numbering nearly fifty members met there every afternoon during the ball-playing season." But it was then strictly an elitist game played only by merchants, lawyers, and doctors, who made it a year-round sport. In the winter they even tried baseball on ice skates.

As the popularity of the game grew, Rochester's public squares were transformed into baseball diamonds to the annoyance of nearby residents. Ministers also questioned the morality of games on the Sabbath. But in time baseball came to be seen as a healthy pastime, leading the *Rochester Democrat and American* to write in 1858: "The exhilaration of green fields and pure air will supplant the morbid and pernicious cravings for tobacco and rum . . . Baseball playing would be a time for fathers and mothers and friends to share a common interest."

I gleaned all of this from the book *Silver Seasons: The Story of the Rochester Red Wings*, written by reporters Jim Mandelaro and Scott Pitoniak. Jim had very thoughtfully given me an autographed copy, realizing while sitting up there in the press box, how ignorant I was about the Red Wings. The book, I also discovered, had a fascinating description of one of Babe Ruth's local appearances with the Yankees in a 1925 exhibition game.

Red Wings' pitcher Harry Weaver was instructed to groove a fastball so the Babe could hit a home run and send the crowd home happy. Being fiercely competitive, Weaver at first refused, but finally relented. "Where do you want it?" the Rochester catcher asked Ruth. "Belt high," said the Babe, and drove the first ball over the scoreboard in right field, so high that it even cleared a row of poplar trees and houses across the street.

Since it was still early in the afternoon when the game against Pawtucket was cancelled, my wife and I decided to skip going back to the hotel and spend the night with friends at their summer home on Lake Canandaigua. They had very kindly called a couple of times to invite us, even sending a map of the network of small roads winding through the wine vineyards, so we wouldn't get lost.

Their place, with its dining patios, waterfront gardens, floating trampoline, and a couple of speedboats (not to mention a washing machine and drier that we badly needed the use of), proved a virtual Eden. We spent the next morning hiking the shoreline. Our host also took us on a short cruise to view the summer mansions facing the lake that were hidden by trees from the road.

Returning to the ballpark that afternoon, I sat in the sun behind first base watching batting practice. The stands were empty, except for a man speaking into a tape recorder a few seats away. Curious about what he was up to, I introduced myself. "I'm Wayne Krivsky," he replied, "assistant general manager of the Twins. At least that's my title," he explained. "I live in Arlington, Texas, and scout the National League."

The conversation finally got around to Liriano, who Wayne apparently missed seeing when the Dominican belonged to San Francisco. "I recommended Joe Nathan," he said. "That was my only part of the multiplayer deal that brought Liriano to the Twins. So I can't take any credit for him. But after seeing his debut with the Rock Cats, I got right on the phone with general manager Terry Ryan and told him how much I liked what I saw."

This was Wayne's first trip to Rochester in 2005, and he said he was eager to see how well Liriano had developed. "Everywhere I go I hear scouts talking about him. Several clubs are trying to make a trade for him. But they're wasting their time."

By 5 PM fans were flocking in for the first game of the make-up doubleheader, still not scheduled to start for another hour. Despite their double loss to Syracuse, the Red Wings were still pressing Buffalo for the division championship. Also, the special pregame show that evening, "Rockin' Ray and the Sky Dogs USA," had helped to further swell attendance. The dogs were remarkable. Standing at home plate, Ray would skim one Frisbee after another out over first base into right field. The dogs would race out and leap into the air and catch them in their mouth without ever missing and then deliver them back to their master. The crowd roared its appreciation.

But it was Liriano who was the real attraction. The announced attendance of 12,248 paid admissions was Frontier Field's second largest crowd of the season. Only the opening-day crowd was bigger. Since all games in minor league doubleheaders are limited to seven innings, everyone expected the Dominican might go the distance, possibly extending his scoreless streak to 33 innings.

Well, in baseball as in life, things don't always go as planned. The omens were bad right from the beginning when Pawtucket's lead off batter Dustin Pedroia lashed out a single. The crowd, of course, had hoped the young left-hander would limit the PawSox to no more than one or two hits during the entire game.

Perhaps it was just a fluke hit, they thought, because Liriano turned right around and struck out designated hitter Mark Bellhorn, a big-league star sent down by the Red Sox to Pawtucket on rehab. It was Bellhorn who proved such a thorn in the side of the Yankees in the 2004 play-offs and World Series. Striking him out was not easy, and the fans cheered when he went down swinging. But then suddenly things got worse. Liriano lost his vaulted control and loaded the bases by walking both Dave Berg and Adam Hyzdun.

It looked to me as if he was hurrying, too eager to get out of the inning and safely back to the dugout where Bobby Cuellar could tell him what he was doing wrong. As soon as he got the ball back from the catcher he stepped on the rubber, ready to throw again. Francisco, my friend, slow down, I said to myself.

He threw two more balls to the next batter, Justin Sherrod, hardly stopping between pitches to glance over at the runners. Now, for sure I expected to see Bobby Cuellar come traipsing out to the mound to slow the Dominican down. But Bobby left him alone as Liriano appeared to regain his rhythm, striking out Sherrod with three successive fastballs. You could almost hear the crowd let out a collective sigh of relief.

The next man up, third baseman Luis Figueroa, known as a cagey batter who rarely struck out, swung and missed at the first two pitches. Surely Liriano was now back on track.

One more strike and there would be two away, making it easy for him to get out of the inning without being scored on.

But Figueroa was not going to be disposed of that easily. In what Jim Mandelaro reported as a "gritty at-bat," he fouled off Liriano's next five pitches, working the count up to 2-2. On Liriano's 10th pitch, a 95-mile-an-hour bullet, Figueroa lined the ball into right field, scoring two runs. That wasn't what the big crowd had come with such excitement to see.

Catcher Shawn Wooten, the next batter, took two quick called strikes, a ball, and then again without swinging took what looked to all the fans at Frontier Field like another fastball right down the middle. Hall of Famer Joe Altobelli, sitting next to me, winced in sympathy for Liriano. "Perfect strike," he said. But that wasn't the way the umpire saw it.

Liriano became visibly upset, shaking his head angrily, figuring he'd finally struck out the side. This time Bobby did come out to calm him down. Liriano regained his composure, and I thought I even detected a slight smile before Bobby left the mound. Apparently, I was wrong. Liriano was still fuming and on the next high, hard pitch, Wooten lashed a long single into left field, driving in the third run of the inning before being thrown out trying to stretch his hit into a double. The crowd sat in stunned silence. Jim Mandelaro said he'd never witnessed such a hush fall over Frontier Field.

Liriano got through the second inning all right on a pair of routine groundouts and a fly ball. In the third inning he was nicked for a single and a double, and in the fourth, for a triple that missed clearing the center-field fence by inches. No more runs scored, but that was enough for acting manager Rich Miller, who replaced him in the fifth inning with reliever Beau Kemp. "I was so mad," the mild-mannered Dominican told me later, "that I felt like hitting somebody."

Fortunately for his win–loss record, Rochester quickly scored three runs, and the lead seesawed back and forth after that, so technically he wasn't charged with the Red Wings' 8-7 defeat. But after the game some of the players, envious of all the publicity Liriano was getting, came up to Bobby grumbling that the star lefty wasn't all he was cracked up to be. "You replay that first inning," Bobby replied angrily, "and you'll see that if it hadn't been for that one bad call this game would have ended differently." Nobody, it seemed, could attack the pitching coach's pet protégé and get away with it.

But the banner headline spread across the front page of the *Democrat and Chronicle*'s sports section the next morning said it all: "LIRIANO'S STREAK IS ENDED." And so was our stay in Rochester.

13

GOOD-BYE ROCK CATS

It was time to revisit the Rock Cats, who were back again in the thick of the play-offs chase following a five-game winning streak. On our way south from Rochester, we decided to detour through Cooperstown for a quick visit to the Baseball Hall of Fame. I'd been there before when our four sons were growing up. But now sheer curiosity was luring me back to locate the cap worn by Steve Grilli, the losing pitcher of Rochester's record-breaking 33-inning game.

The scenic route—and we had become partial to those—took us through Watkins Glen at the foot of Lake Seneca. We stopped there for a sandwich at the picnic grounds in front of Montour Falls, or She-Qua-Ga (Tumbling Falls), as a historic marker indicated the Indians called it. The sign also revealed that "In about 1820, Louis Phillippe, who later became King of France, made a sketch of the falls that is now in the Louvre." Helen also quickly sketched the falls after finishing her sandwich, and we decided that we'd have to compare the two sketches the next time we were in Paris. A drought, however, had reduced the Tumbling Falls to a wispy flow, barely wetting the sheer rock behind it.

We spent the night with friends in Cooperstown at their cabin on Lake Otsego encircled by the foothills of the Catskills. At sunset the wind died and the lake became mirror-flat, showing why James Fenimore Cooper named it "glimmerglass." A lonely kayak cut a clean furrow in the lake's surface. That stunning sight was the backdrop for our cocktail hour before dinner.

To save time the next morning, we decided to skip pursuing Steve Grilli's cap and head straight for New Britain, opting for thruways this time wherever we could. Arriving at the ballpark before batting practice, I found the Rock Cats ready and eager to take on the Erie SeaWolves in the final two of a three-game series. Justin Olson had already won his ninth game, a spot start against the Harrisburg Senators on August 12. And since enough time had elapsed, I hoped he might get the chance to start one of the Erie games.

I also hoped to catch up with Jim Rantz once again, to wheedle out of him if possible, the chances of Liriano being called up by the Twins on September 1, the date the major-league rosters would be expanded to 40 players. The last time we'd talked, he spoke glowingly of the Dominican's chances of perhaps even joining the Twins' starting rotation.

What convinced him that Liriano was probably ready, he'd explained, was not just the young left-hander's fastball, or the fact that he'd developed a biting slider and a changeup that could snap the wrists of the opposing batters. It was the movement of his fastball.

"Every pitcher is geared to velocity," Rantz had said. "Sure, Liriano can throw 95, 96, or even 97. But his fastball also has life. It can sink, it can rise, or it can run. That's what makes him so hard to hit. Pitchers who throw a straight fastball better find another way to hold it," he warned. It occurred to me that he might have been referring to Olson, whose fastballs were all-too-frequently blasted out of the park.

Jim had also been very admiring of Liriano's "command and control," as he called his mound presence. "Hitting," he continued, "is all about timing. If you can throw off the batter's timing, that's the name of the game. And Liriano has a natural ability for doing that with his changeup." Unfortunately, Rantz had already gone back to Minneapolis when I arrived in New Britain. But Rick Knapp, the Twins' minor-league pitching coordinator, was there. He thought Liriano was definitely destined for Minneapolis, unless the Red Wings broke out of their losing streak and gained a spot in the play-offs. "All I can say is, this kid is way beyond his years in maturity. And I mean both on and off the field."

A good-natured bear-of-a-man, Rick liked to inject a little humor into his comments. "You know, first, we usually have to teach these young pitchers about beer," he said. "Next we have to teach them about cars. Then we have to teach them about girls. Finally, when they've learned all those things, they're ours to work with. But all Liriano's interested in is baseball." That, I told him, was my impression too. Whenever I interviewed him the conversation always reverted to baseball.

"Seriously," Rick added, "there's only one problem with Liriano. I think he's a perfection player. He strikes out one batter, then he's got to strike the next one." Rick then went into a long soliloquy dismissing the importance of strikeouts.

"We don't want our guys trying for strikeouts all the time," he declared. "We want them to put themselves in a strikeout position. Then if they have an opportunity to strike the guy out, go ahead, take a shot. But there are so many factors involved. Whether the batter's going to swing at a ball in the dirt, or swing at a ball over his head. Those are factors a pitcher just can't control. The strikeout is more of a result of the pitcher putting himself in a good position and then getting lucky."

I always figured the more the strikeouts the merrier. Certainly everybody else in the Twins' management hierarchy seemed overjoyed with all the "Ks" Liriano was putting on their scorecards.

It was nice to hear Rick express his satisfaction with the recent performance of the Rock Cats' pitchers. The team had returned home from a four-game sweep of Harrisburg, and after beating Erie last night, was only three-and-a-half games out of a play-off spot. Still, making the play-offs remained a long shot. As pitching coach Stew Cliburn warned, "We're chasing good teams and we've only got 19 games left to play."

Knowing my interest in Olson, Rick also praised his dual

contributions as starter and reliever. "He's done a good job for the Rock Cats," he said. But Rick sounded even more impressed with the way Glenn Perkins and Nick Blackburn had developed. "You know both of them came up from Fort Myers in midseason. We even sent them up to Rochester to pitch a couple of games for the Red Wings, before bringing them back to New Britain."

Olson hadn't been given that opportunity, but I found him in good spirits nevertheless. He'd forgotten all about his disastrous start against Trenton that ruined the day his wife and parents came to watch him pitch. Like his teammates, he was looking ahead, eager to take on the SeaWolves in pursuit of a possible play-off berth.

"You'll find me out in the bull pen," he said after greeting me as an old friend. "Stew's already told me I'm not going to start again until August 19 down in Bowie." Feeling no pressure, he promised to come to the ballpark early the next afternoon so we could talk. That, I realized, was going to be the last time for us to get together, since he'd be heading back for Illinois as soon as the Eastern League's regular season ended on August 31.

I wanted to find out how he regarded his summer in Double-A. Was it a learning experience? Did he improve a lot? Did he gain confidence? Is he still chasing the dream of playing in the big leagues? Liriano could clearly see how his career was shaping up. But could Olson?

"Switching back and forth between relieving and starting hasn't really bothered me," Justin said. "In either case, I've learned you just go out there and pitch one inning at a time. Any starter that tells you he's going to throw six or seven innings doesn't know that. He may not last one inning. Still, he's got to pace himself and keep a few bullets in reserve without letting things lapse."

Groping to define the differences between his two roles, he added, "Pitching out of the bull pen requires a little more adrenaline. You come in cold in the middle of a game and you're going head-to-head with a batter you may not know anything about. That's why I like it when I hear Stew say, 'You're my middle-innings guy.' I know he's counting on me to keep us in the game until he sends in the closer to nail it down."

Perhaps it was as a middle-innings guy that Olson visualized himself going to the big leagues. There's a demand for pitchers who can fill that special role. In any case, it was obvious that he'd already taken stock of what the season in Double-A had done for him. "I feel that my slider has come along pretty well," he said. "I can now throw it for strikes. That and fastball command were my two main goals for this year. But I feel a little doubtful about my changeup. It's still not good enough to rely on. And I guess my ERA could come down a little. Other than that, I think my numbers are good."

Then I broached what I worried might be a sensitive subject. "How do you feel about your old friend Francisco's great success in Triple-A? From what Rick Knapp tells me, he's probably headed for the Twins."

"That's great," Justin replied. "We're both trying to achieve the same thing. We started out on the Miracle together. But let's face it, he's got better stuff."

There he goes again, I thought. Olson's modesty never

fails to surface in any conversation. That's just his nature. He always has to credit the other guy. If he pitched a good game, it's the hitters that won it. If he lost, it was his fault even though the infielders may have booted a couple of grounders, resulting in several unearned runs.

Olson then went on to remind me of his friendship with Liriano. "The language barrier was always a bit of a challenge," he said. "And off the field the Latin players tended to do their own thing. Liriano was the only one of them I hung around with. We got along well."

As he continued to talk, the conversation became more of a stream-of-consciousness venting of his aspirations. "My goal is to pitch up in Rochester next year," he admitted. "The brand of ball there, they tell me, is pretty much the same. But if that doesn't happen, I don't know. And as I've said before, I'd like to play winter ball in Venezuela. That would give me additional time to work on my changeup before spring training. But given the innings I've thrown here, the Twins probably won't think it's necessary. Otherwise, I'll be back home painting houses. I talked to my old boss the other night. He says, 'come on back.' His name is Ron, but they call him Ronbo. Actually, he was my Little League coach and sponsored our team. Ronbo's Fine Painting was its name."

I was disappointed that Olson wasn't summoned from the bull pen in either of the final two games against the Sea-Wolves, both of which the Rock Cats won. They, nevertheless, were exciting contests, igniting manager Stan Cliburn's hopes of pulling off another one of his August miracles. In the first game it was the spectacular hitting of Danny Matienzo—a double, a homer, and three RBIs—that resulted in a 7-4 victory. The second night it was a two-hit pitching gem by Lavale Speigner that shut out the SeaWolves 2-0.

General Manager Bill Dowling was elated. "It looks like this is going to be a typical Stan Cliburn finish," he said. "Given the ups and downs of the season it would be awesome if we ended up in the play-offs." Then suddenly stricken with a dose of reality, he added, "The bad news is that the two teams we still have to play are behind us in the league standings." But nothing could deflate Bill. "It looks like our attendance should hit 330,000," he bragged. "That's about 20,000 more than last year."

I found it hard leaving the Rock Cats at this crucial moment. The players had become my friends. The season-long association with Bill, his brother Bob, the Cliburn twins, and particularly Justin, had been a wonderful experience. Next year I was sure most of them would be scattered: Stan very possibly up in Rochester as manager, Stew probably somewhere else, and Justin back in New Britain, up in Rochester, or even home in Oak Park. He was the big question mark.

Of course I would follow the team on the Internet through the remaining games of the season and keep in touch with Olson by phone. But it wouldn't be the same.

Yet, the Red Wings were also coming down the homestretch of their season. And I was determined to see Liriano pitch what might be his final minor-league game against the PawSox on Saturday, August 20. There was no choice but to bid the Rock Cats good-bye and hit the road.

14

THE REAL MCCOY

There is no direct route from New Britain to McCoy Stadium, home of the PawSox. After crossing the Connecticut River at Middletown, the roads zig and zag northeast through the "Thread City" of Willimantic, Connecticut, to South Killingly at the Rhode Island border, and then on into Providence, and finally a few miles north to Pawtucket.

The empty red-brick textile mills along the way stand as decaying monuments to the pre–World War II days, when the looms of New England employed thousands of Irish immigrant women. Many of the mills are finally being converted into office buildings, high-tech plants, and condominiums, giving this part of New England new economic vitality. But the transition is slow and many towns are still worn-looking and in dire need of perking up.

We stopped for a late lunch at a diner on the edge of Pawtucket. From the waitress we learned that besides the PawSox, the city also boasts of having the Slaterettes, the first all-girls and women's baseball club in the United States and the sister team of the Slaters, as the PawSox once were called. A hefty woman with thick wrists, the waitress apparently was one of the Slaterettes' star hitters. "We're playing tonight," she said. "You and your wife should come."

Checking in at McCoy Stadium, I found that Bill Wanless, the PawSox vice president for public relations, had my credentials all ready. Liriano was not scheduled to pitch until the next night, Saturday, but I wanted to go to tonight's game to get acquainted with the reporters in the press box and, if possible, interview Ron Johnson, the PawSox manager, and Mike Griffin, the pitching coach. With a little luck I figured I might run into Francisco in the clubhouse, although I knew he'd be charting the PawSox batters.

The game was a heartbreaker for the Red Wings. They were coasting along, leading 3-0 going into the bottom of the seventh inning, when the PawSox suddenly came alive and rallied for three runs to tie the score. Neither team scored in the eighth. And with two outs and two strikes on Pawtucket's left-fielder Dave Berg in the bottom of the ninth, it looked like the game was going into extra innings. Berg fouled off two more pitches, then lashed a single into left field, scoring shortstop Luis Figueroa, and sending the local fans home happy with a walk-off victory.

After the game I went down to the clubhouse to interview both Johnson and Griffin. I was curious to find out if they'd devised a strategy for beating Liriano. "You saw, didn't you, that we got three runs off him in the first inning in Rochester last Monday," declared the manager, an outwardly gruff but good-humored man. The manager conveyed the impression that he thought Liriano might be overrated. "His numbers are good," he said, "but numbers down at this level can be deceiving."

As he explained it, his strategy was pretty simple. "When you face a guy like that, you've got to be patient. Make him throw a lot and run up his pitch count. Last Monday, we made him throw like 60 times in the first two innings."

Johnson, obviously, didn't want to lavish a lot of praise on a member of the opposition. "Sure, I'll admit Liriano may be the best prospect I've seen on another team. But I'll stand by my own guys. We've got some pretty good ones like Abe Alvarez. He's only 22 and has really good stuff."

The PawSox pitching coach was a little more magnanimous. Though he, too, didn't feel the Dominican would be too hard to beat if the PawSox hitters were in good form. "The kid showed us the other night that he had pretty good mound presence," Mike said. "I mean after we jumped on him for three runs. From what I also saw he can get his breaking stuff over for strikes. But when you're that young you need more mound time to hone your skills."

So clearly the two PawSox field bosses were not intimidated by the Red Wings' young left-hander's record. Let's see what happens tomorrow night, I thought. They just don't appreciate his talents.

The next morning Helen and I rose early with the idea

of visiting the Rhode Island School of Design Museum. We were staying at the Holiday Inn in Providence along with the Red Wings, and it was just a short drive across the river to the adjacent Rhode Island School of Design and Brown University campuses. Both are built into the side of a steep hill, providing strenuous exercise for the students climbing up and down between classes.

The museum's remarkable exhibit of ancient Asian artifacts particularly interested my wife, who'd worked for an Oriental antiques dealer in Hong Kong in the 1970s, when I was covering China and Vietnam for *Time* magazine. Featured at the museum was a 10-foot-high, gold-encrusted Buddha, said to be the largest in the United States. Of course, it would have been dwarfed by the enormous Smiling Buddha we'd seen many times in Bangkok.

From the museum we took a stroll around Brown's magnificent grounds, shaded by huge oaks and maples, but almost empty because summer school was not in session. We stopped for lunch at a campus café with descriptions of 50 or 60 soup-and-sandwich combinations scribbled on the walls, before heading out to McCoy Stadium in time for batting practice.

The PawSox have been a Red Sox farm team for 35 years. And although McCoy Stadium is ancient compared to most of the International League ballparks, having been erected in 1942, it was rebuilt in 1992 and enlarged again in 1999 to accommodate more than 10,000 fans.

I was surprised to find Rick Knapp there. He also had driven up from New Britain to get another look at Liriano. Sitting in the visitors' dugout he launched into an interesting discussion of the Twins' philosophy for developing young players. "Sometimes," he said, "it's not a matter of concentrating on the guy with the most ability or highest profile, but the one who's going to fit best into the major-league team's mold. That may mean being quiet, paying attention, and not being flashy." Olson certainly fit that description. And so did Liriano, except for his increasingly high profile.

"We have a plan for each pitcher," Rick continued. "In Liriano's case we identified early on some of the delivery issues that needed to be fixed. We helped him, but mainly he helped himself. There were also some little things, like when the batter stepped out of the box to delay him, he became upset. That's an attitude thing and we taught him to ignore it."

"You know," Rick concluded, "Sometimes I think my job sucks, telling kids what they're doing wrong."

By 6:30 PM the stands were almost completely filled, not unusual for a Saturday night. But even in Pawtucket where the fans came hoping to see Liriano get beaten, he was still a big attraction. Some 1,500 Boy Scouts and Girl Scouts had been invited to the game. They marched into the stadium two abreast, waving their troop banners aloft, and arraying themselves in an arc around the edge of the infield. For 20 minutes they serenaded the crowd with patriotic songs. Then they marched back off the field and filed into the stands.

I watched Liriano warm up in the bull pen out in right field. His movements were fluid and effortless. Whatever those "delivery issues" were that Rick spoke of, they appeared to me to have been corrected. Completing his warm-up, he walked briskly back to the dugout, eager to get out on the mound and fire his first pitch.

Rochester jumped right on Anastacio Martinez, the PawSox right-hander, scoring one run on two hits and a stolen base in the first inning.

Liriano strode gracefully to the mound, glancing up momentarily at the huge crowd, and then focused on the first batter, Dustin Pedroia. On the second pitch he lined out the first baseman. But the next man up, Rochester's nemesis, Dave Berg, beat out an infield hit. That didn't faze Francisco, who—throwing 96- and 97-mile-an-hour fastballs—struck out Adam Hyzdu and Kelly Shoppach to end the inning.

Spending little time on the mound between pitches, Liriano appeared to be a well-oiled, smooth-running machine. After a scratch hit, an infield groundout, a pop-up to the catcher, and a strikeout took care of the home team in the second inning. Pawtucket's third inning ended just as quickly with a groundout, another infield hit, and a double play. But it was the fourth and fifth innings where Liriano really shone. Alternating 96- and 97-mile-an-hour fastballs with devastating 85- and 86-mile-an-hour changeups and sliders, he struck the next six men in a row, a feat that hadn't been accomplished by a Red Wings' pitcher in more than a year. And not a ball had been hit out of the infield until an easy fly to center field in the sixth inning, after which Liriano struck out two more. He added one more strikeout in the seventh, giving him a total of 12, before being replaced in the eighth by reliever Beau Kemp.

"He's got a great arm," declared Luis Figueroa, the only PawSox batter Liriano didn't strike out.

I was surprised that none of the Pawtucket and Providence reporters went down to the clubhouse to interview Liriano after the game. If he'd lost, I suppose, that would have been more of a story for them. I'd never seen the Dominican so outwardly happy, grinning like a kid with ice packs still taped to his shoulder, and exclaiming to anybody who'd listen: "My changeup and my slider were working real good."

When I asked him if he wanted to hang in there and pitch the whole game, he shook his head. "Bobby came out to the mound in the seventh inning and asked if I could keep on throwing for two more innings. I told him I was getting tired"—a rare admission for Liriano, who takes such pride in his physical condition.

Bobby, too, was just glowing about his protégé's performance. "I went out there to the mound because he'd thrown a wild pitch and given up a base on balls, and I thought he was suddenly trying too hard, getting away from his regular motion. He was doing things that he knows get him in trouble. So I just wanted to calm him down."

There was no stopping Bobby, who was excited that Liriano had given up only one base on balls and four hits. "He only threw 93 pitches," the pitching coach exclaimed. "And he was still lighting up the pitch-speed sign with 96s and 97s in the sixth and seventh innings. You see, once he's in the groove he gets stronger and stronger."

Of course that's not what happened in Rochester against this same team five days earlier. Liriano felt so bad about the way he'd pitched that night that Bobby claimed he followed him around all the next day like a lost puppy. Even the Red Wings hitting coach Rich Miller, filling in as manager, couldn't get over his morose behavior. "You'd have thought he was having a bad dream," Rich said.

I wondered what the PawSox pitching coach would say now having seen the Dominican's dazzling performance. Unfortunately, Mike Griffin had already dressed and gone home. But I'd already decided to come back for the Sunday afternoon game and figured I could catch him then.

Mike was out in the bull pen in left field warming up a pitcher when I arrived on Sunday. He's the hands-on kind of coach who likes doing that, and by his own admission, also enjoys throwing batting practice and engaging in all of his team's calisthenics. When he spotted me coming, he tossed his mitt to one of the players and motioned to a wooden bench in the back of the bull pen.

Right from the start it was obvious that Liriano had made quite an impression. "You can talk about his slider, you can talk about his changeup, you can talk about his 95-, 96-, 97-mile-an-hour fastballs," the PawSox pitching coach exclaimed. "But you know what surprises me? It's his presence, the way he carries himself on the mound."

I couldn't get over Mike's change of attitude since yesterday. He was now so enthusiastic, you'd have thought he was talking about one of his own pitchers. "There's no need to comment on his stuff," he continued. "His stuff is there. He's got three pitches at the major-league level. Three well-above-average major-league pitches."

I could tell the PawSox pitching coach must have been watching every one of Liriano's movements and gestures. "He got himself in a couple of jams last night," Mike admitted. "But he turned around and made some quality pitches to get out of them. You can talk about a pitcher who goes out and shuts the other team down. That's impressive. But show me a pitcher that gets in trouble and then battles his way out of it to give his team a chance to win; that's even more impressive."

For a minute, Mike stopped to praise his own pitcher last night, Anastacio Martinez. "We'd lost three starters," he said. "Martinez came out of the bull pen and gave us five good innings. That's huge for a ballplayer in my estimation." Mike's comment suddenly made me think of Olson, who'd been called out of the bull pen so many times to make a spot start. I wondered if Stew Cliburn had been that appreciative of his effort.

"You know, I've only seen Liriano twice, last Monday and last night," Mike declared. "But from what I saw he has great body control. In other words his body's under control during his entire delivery. That's great. That's what a pitcher has to have."

He pointed across to the other side of the stadium where Liriano was jogging. "Look at him," he said. "There he is running laps the morning after he pitched. He's thinking about his body. All the time pitchers have to think about their body to keep on the five-day rotation." Looking at the 48-year-old pitching coach's sinewy figure, I assumed he took very good care of his.

Mike had almost run out of nice things to say. "I know Liriano's got good demeanor on the mound," he added, also indicating that the interview was about over. "I hear he doesn't screw around off the field either. That's unheard of for a young pitcher."

As I walked back to the clubhouse, Liriano had just finished running his laps and was resting in the visitors' dugout. I told him that the PawSox pitching coach had been very impressed with the way he pitched last night. "Who was your first baseball coach?" I asked, wondering if it could have been a Dominican player now in the big leagues, and a name I would recognize.

"My coach in San Cristobal when I was 10-years-old was Juan Balera," he said, or at least that's the way I heard him pronounce the name. "He was a good coach, and I still talk to him on the phone. He got me hitting pretty good, but I was so slow running the bases he called me *la tortuga* (the tortoise)." Liriano had never mentioned his coach before. But then new details about his life kept emerging each time we talked.

The conversation reverted back to the game last night. "I was feeling pretty good," he said. "I was throwing hard, but I never look at the (pitch-speed) sign. I don't pay attention to that. Some days I don't feel 100 percent. Like last Monday, I didn't feel that good. But if we're going to get in the play-offs, I think I must feel good every time."

I knew everybody in the Red Wings organization would agree with that. The fact that they were in contention was due a great deal to his 8-1 win-loss record. "I think we can make it," he added proudly. "We're only one game behind Buffalo. They lost last night."

"How come you couldn't fan Figueroa last night?" I asked, trying get a rise out of this serious young man. "He was the only one you didn't strike out."

"Figueroa is the kind of guy that's hard to strike out,"

he replied, not realizing that I was kidding. "Did you see, he almost hit a home run in the ninth inning."

That was true. With two outs, Figueroa hit a ball over the right-field fence barely a foot to the right of the foul pole. By then Travis Bowyer, the closer, was pitching for Rochester. But had that ball been fair, it would have erased Liriano's great victory.

"Figueroa is a very tough batter," he replied. "He fouls off a lot of pitches. But he doesn't scare me."

It never occurred to me that any batter could scare this commanding left-hander. "Have you ever been scared out there on the mound?" I asked.

"Not really," he replied. "After the Giants signed me, I came to the United States and pitched in relief. They had me throw an inning against Oakland. Not in the season, but in spring training. I was only 17, so maybe I was scared then. But I got 'em all out. That's when they decided for sure to make me a pitcher."

Here, I'd spent a good part of the season following the Dominican and had never heard that story before. I was sure there were many more that I'd missed—exciting moments that shaped his career—that I would now only read about if he got called up by the Twins.

We sat in silence in the dugout for a few more minutes before saying good-bye. "I'll be calling you from time to time," I said. For the first time I felt that Francisco Liriano was not just the pitcher I'd picked to follow and write about. He, like Olson, had finally become a friend.

15

ROOKIE OF THE YEAR

Liriano's pitching gem against Pawtucket triggered a burst of national publicity for the young left-hander. *The New York Times, USA Today,* and Baseball America's *Daily Dish* all featured stories on his rapid climb towards the majors. "Amidst the debate as to who is the best pitching prospect in the International League," wrote Chris Kline in the *Daily Dish,* "Liriano is quickly ending that discussion."

The writer then went on to describe in glowing terms Liriano's overpowering repertoire. "He throws three pitches for strikes—his fastball tops out at 97 mph. He complements it with a hard-breaking 86-88 mph slider, and a changeup he drops off at 82-83 with same easy arm action as his fastball. He's tough because his fastball might be his third best pitch."

In conclusion the article claimed, "Liriano has nothing left to prove in the International League; he's ready to join Johan Santana in Minnesota's rotation."

That had already become obvious to many of the players and coaches of the opposing teams, who almost cried foul when the Red Wings sent Liriano to the mound to face them. "The bottom line is that this guy doesn't belong in this league," claimed Buffalo's manager Marty Brown.

Fred Bierman of *The New York Times*, I thought, delivered the ultimate accolade: "Finally healthy this season, Liriano has emerged as one of the top pitchers in the Twins organization, if not in the entire minor leagues."

But the season was not yet over. As it turned out Liriano had two more turns on the Red Wings' rotation, trying to keep them in contention for the play-offs. Returning to Rochester's Frontier Field just two games out of first place, the Dominican beat the troublesome Ottawa Lynx 5-2. He struck out nine without walking a batter in seven innings. But he wasn't as sharp as usual. The Lynx sluggers, who had caused him difficulty before, got to him again for eight hits and two earned runs, causing Bobby Cuellar to make a couple of trips to the mound, the first one after the Dominican uncorked a wild pitch, something he rarely does.

"You know, these are learning experiences for him," the pitching coach told me after the game. "Ottawa's more of a running team, a team that has many big swingers and puts the ball in play." Still Bobby sounded proud of the way his protégé performed. "Francisco kept his head and didn't walk anybody," he said. "Yes, they got some hits off him, but then those guys give everybody a pretty good battle."

Bobby's second trip to the mound that evening came in the seventh inning with two outs. "Liriano was almost up to his maximum number of pitches," the pitching coach explained. " 'This is your last batter,' " I told him. So he threw his 106th pitch and the guy hit it pretty good, a screaming line drive, but right at the left-fielder. You could say he was a little lucky the ball got caught. But that's part of the game."

Liriano's next turn to pitch came in an away game against first-place Buffalo. Just 13 days earlier Rochester had tied their western New York State rivals for the division lead. But since then the Red Wings had gone into a near fatal swoon, losing eight games while the Bisons won 11. Even though the Red Wings' fortunes had plummeted, and they were almost out of contention, the challenge of a last-ditch effort was still there when the Dominican took the mound in Dunn Tire Park on August 30.

As it turned out he would face two enemies that night: the hard-hitting Bisons, and the remnants of the harder-hitting Hurricane Katrina. The forecast was for heavy rain, but there were no days left in the schedule for a make-up game.

What started as a steady drizzle kept getting worse with every inning. Still, Liriano didn't feel threatened by either the weather or the Buffalo batters. And why should he? The last time he'd faced them at Frontier Field, he'd held them to one scratch hit in seven innings, while striking out a record 13.

Once again the left-hander looked sharp, throwing with easy looping arm motions. The rain didn't appear to affect either his slider or his changeup, as he mixed them up with his overpowering fastball to keep the Bisons fanning the air. After two scoreless innings, Rochester jumped ahead in the third on first baseman Garrett Jones's towering home run into the right-field stands, his 22nd of the year.

In spite of the rain, Liriano held on to the one-run lead through the fourth inning. In the fifth, Red Wings left-fielder Josh Rabe missed by inches hitting his 11th home run with a lead off shot down the left-field line that almost clipped the foul pole. He eventually walked, raced to third on catcher Rob Bowen's single, and scored on right-fielder Todd Dunwoody's groundout. That gave Liriano a slightly more comfortable two-run lead as the Bisons came to bat in the bottom of the fifth.

The rain was now pelting down, and according to Bobby Cuellar, Liriano found it difficult to grip the ball. The result: a pair of solo homers by Jason Dubois and Dusty Wathan. "I could see he was overthrowing," Wathan said. "I figured if I just kept swinging hard enough one might eventually go out of the park, and it did." Joe Inglett followed with a single. With two outs and Liriano still clinging to a 2-2 tie, a wild throw by third baseman Luis Maza sailed down the right-field line, allowing Inglett to race all the way home from first. A tumbling slide across the plate through the slop gave Buffalo a 3-2 lead.

"I'm sure the error energized Buffalo," said manager Rich Miller. "Liriano was pitching well, and then boom! The first home runs anybody hit off him in almost two months."

It energized Rochester too. For a moment in the sixth inning, after a single and a walk put Red Wings' runners on first and second with one out, it looked like the game might be tied again. But Rochester failed to score, delighting the waterlogged crowd of almost 13,000 that had braved the foul weather on Fans Appreciation Night.

Liriano was still throwing hard in the bottom of the sixth, racking up his ninth and tenth strikeouts. But it was the weather, not the Bison batters that delivered the final knockout punch. What began as a drizzle ended as a down-pour, forcing the game to be shortened to six-and-one-half innings, and giving Buffalo a 3-2 victory.

The loss was only Liriano's second against nine wins. There were three other contests in which he was not in-volved in the decision. Usually a hard loser, known to mope around for a day or two after a defeat, Liriano came off the mound this time to hear some good news. The International League managers, coaches, and media had voted him Rookie of the Year. "Isn't that amazing!" exclaimed Dan Mason, Rochester's general manager. "The kid spends half the season down in Double-A, throwing for New Britain. Then he comes up here and in a little more than two months sets the league on fire."

That honor was soon topped by still another from *USA Today*. The newspaper named Liriano Minor-League Player of the Year, the first Rochester pitcher ever to be so hon-ored. It cited his season total of 204 strikeouts, the most in the minors; his phenomenal 1.78 earned run average with the Red Wings; and the fact that he held his International League opponents to a puny .177 batting average.

Bobby Cuellar couldn't contain his excitement. "He's done a wonderful thing for baseball," he declared. "Imagine a young kid like him being chosen the best minor-league player. Not just the best pitcher, but the best player, during his first half season in Triple-A."

With the Red Wings eliminated from the play-off chase, I felt it was time for me to turn my attention back to New Britain and the Rock Cats. Unfortunately, it turned out that not only had the Red Wings gone into a late-season swoon, but their Double-A brothers, while on a less precipitous slide, had virtually eliminated themselves from the play-offs in their league as well. Speaking from his Minneapolis office, Jim Rantz, the Twins minor-league boss, issued what struck me as a Pollyanna statement: "We were in a situation in both leagues where we challenged the leader," he announced to the media. "The excitement was there. But it just didn't happen."

In fact, when I'd left New Britain on August 18, the excitement was still very much there. The players, the coaches, and especially the fans, were counting on manager Stan Cliburn to pull off another one of his August miracles as he had a couple of times in the past. But by the end the month, New Britain was still hovering around the 500 mark and clearly out of contention. Besides, Trenton just kept on winning, making it impossible for them to be overtaken even for a wild-card spot.

When I telephoned Justin Olson as he and his teammates were about to disband for the winter, he couldn't conceal his disappointment. "It was kind of a bummer," he said. "We really had a chance to make the play-offs. We did everything we could. But we just kept slipping behind."

I realized that for him the season had just sort of petered

out. On August 19, he'd started against Bowie, the team he'd beaten so handily back in July. And although he was not the loser, he gave up five runs in four innings, including his 17th home run of the season. "I felt really bad," he said. "Like I'd let everybody down."

But he made amends during his final two appearances. Coming out of the bull pen first against the Reading Phillies, and then against the Norwich Navigators, he held them both hitless. "I seem to do better in relief," he added, with what I thought sounded like a sorrowful note for not having established himself as a reliable starter.

There were only two games against the Akron Aeros left when we talked. I think Justin hoped to get called in for a couple more innings of relief. But his shoulder flared up, making the end of the season even more of a downer. Stew kept him on the sidelines. "Hey, we're out of the play-offs," the pitching coach told him. "There's no use of your throwing in anger."

I also gleaned from our conversation that Justin felt a little unsettled as he faced "returning to the real world," as he called going home to Oak Park. "Next week I'll start painting again," he said. "And I'll be doing some stuff for my Mom. She did sell her house, so I'll help her move."

Yet, it was clear that baseball and not house painting was still foremost on his mind. "I talked to Jim Rantz," Justin said. "He told me they were pleased that I'd thrown 109 innings this year. However, if I wanted to play winter ball he said they'd let me. But you know, spring training starts around March 10, and that's going to come pretty fast."

I asked Olson how he felt about all the honors being

heaped on Liriano, knowing that there isn't an iota of envy in his heart. "I can't believe the Twins haven't called him up," he replied. "It looked to me like they needed him more in their stretch-run than the Red Wings did."

Justin was right about Minnesota's pitching staff. In the three previous years, the guys on rotation had operated with smooth efficiency in August, helping the Twins to win consecutive American League Central Division titles. Frustrated this year, trying to overtake Cleveland and the White Sox, the rotation fell apart. The sniping and backbiting got so bad that a couple of the starters were in open revolt, unable to conceal their fury against manager Ron Gardenhire. And the dissention wasn't limited to the pitchers. Two of the other players let a personal vendetta almost come to blows.

It was in the midst of that friction-filled atmosphere that Liriano joined the Twins on September 2. Of course nothing, it was assumed, could spoil the thrill for him of a chance to pitch in the majors, even though it was not his nature to show much emotion. To illustrate the point, Red Wings acting manager Rich Miller told me a funny story about how the deadpan Dominican responded to the news that he was being called up.

"Any time one of our guys goes to the majors," Rich explained, "we ask him to sign a baseball before he leaves. We have a glass case full of those signed balls. So I called Liriano in, and I said, 'I need you to sign this baseball for me.' He looked at me like I was crazy. 'Yes,' I told him, 'I need you to autograph this ball. We ask all the guys to do that who get called up to the big leagues.'

"Liriano signed the ball, but it didn't seem to register. I

looked at him and said, 'Well, you're going up.' He still looked at me with a blank face. I said, 'Yes, you're going to the Twins tomorrow morning.'

" 'Oh, I am?' he said. That was his reaction.

"I suppose when you're as good as he is you know what to expect," Rich said, clearly disappointed not to have elicited any excitement out of his star left-hander. "It's not as dramatic as when you figure maybe you've got only an outside chance of making the big leagues." Rich then described how infielder Glenn Williams reacted to the news that he'd been called up earlier in the season.

"Williams was an undrafted Australian kid who played for their Olympic team," Rich explained. "He'd been kicking around the minors for 12 years, in both the Braves' and Blue Jays' farm systems, before we signed him as a free agent. When I told him he was going up, he couldn't believe it. 'You're kidding!' he yelled. 'Are you sure?' Then I thought he was going to cry. You know, it was a great thrill for me seeing his reaction. Liriano didn't even smile."

I couldn't tell if Bobby Cuellar was happy or heartbroken with the news of Liriano's departure. It was a wrench for him losing his star left-hander even though there were only four games left to play. They'd become very close, probably because Bobby spoke fluent Spanish. But also because he'd helped the Dominican a lot.

"Do you think he'll be back here next year for more seasoning?" I asked. The pitching coach looked at me like I was crazy. "Him, come back here? He's better than most of the guys they have up there."

He then told me sort of wistfully how he'd gone to the

hotel to say good-bye to Liriano just before he left. "I be-lieve he was happy," Bobby surmised, "though with him it's hard to tell. I think he expected to stay until our season was over. So maybe in that sense he was surprised."

"Did you give him any last minute advice?" I asked.

"You know him," Bobby answered. "I think you saw what a good person he is and how much talent he has. There isn't much I could tell him. All I said is, 'Go out there and be Liriano. Be yourself. Sometimes when you get to the big leagues, they want you to throw like somebody else. And then you try, and it doesn't work. Just go out there and do your best. That'll be good enough.'"

16

"WELCOME TO
THE BIG LEAGUES"

During his first three days in Minneapolis, Liriano warmed the bench in the bull pen. He didn't seem either awed or excited by the prospect of being called on at any moment to step out into the center of the 45,423-seat Hubert H. Humphrey Metrodome and start throwing to big-league sluggers he'd never faced before. And he didn't give even a glimmer of a smile when the other relief pitchers, following the Twins' traditional rookie initiation, made him wear a Barbie Doll backpack out there in the pen.

I'd finally come to understand this left-hander's calm and collected mien. His deadpan expression didn't mean that he wasn't carefully weighing every situation. Or that he wasn't excited or scared. Jim Rantz claimed, "From the moment Liriano first arrived in Minneapolis, he typically showed no emotion at all. But I think he was smiling on the inside when I told he him he might get a couple of starts before the season's over." Jim Rantz got it right. It was always what was going on inside the Dominican that mattered.

Manager Ron Gardenhire had promised he wouldn't use Liriano "unless the contest was out of reach and it was a low-pressure situation." Finally, on September 5, Labor Day, with the Twins losing 6-0 to the Texas Rangers in the ninth inning, the situation was right. Gardenhire obviously had given up winning the game, and had almost conceded the wild-card spot in the American League pennant race as well. But the holiday crowd was full of anticipation. For several innings they'd been shouting for Liriano. At last they were going to get to see the highly touted rookie, his 97-mph fastball and arsenal of other pitches. They cheered him as he strode in to the mound.

His first pitch was a strike. The fans roared their approval. Lead off batter Gary Matthews, Jr., whose dad played for the San Francisco Giants, Atlanta, and a few other big-league clubs, then worked the count up to three and one. Hoping to smoke a second strike right past him, Liriano let fly with another bullet.

A Double-A, or even Triple-A, batter might have waited to hear if the ump called, "Ball four!" or for another more tempting pitch. Not Matthews. He leaned into it, and with a mighty swing hit a mammoth home run to the rear seats in left field, 438-feet away. When asked exactly how far that ball traveled, Jim Rantz quipped, "We don't know. It's still going."

The crowd sat in stunned silence. To his credit, Liriano then retired the rest of the side in order, striking out the last two batters, while gaining a ripple of applause.

"Welcome to the big leagues," pitching coach Rick Anderson greeted the rookie as he grimly entered the clubhouse. "Oh my!" manager Gardenhire exclaimed. "If you're going to give up a homer, you might as well give up one like that. It was so long the fan who caught it couldn't even throw it back onto the field."

None of those little jibes got a rise out of the Dominican. But when he opened his locker the next day and looked inside he couldn't restrain a smile. His uniform was gone. All that was there was the leather covering of a baseball with the stitches pulled out. A note pinned to it said, "Here's the souvenir ball that Gary Matthews knocked the cover off."

The day after the Matthews' blast, I telephoned Liriano. It was noon but he was still in his room at the Metrodome Holiday Inn and sounded a little groggy. "How's it going up there in the big leagues?" I asked jovially, feigning ignorance of his rude baptism by fire.

"Pretty good," he said. "The people cheered when I came in to pitch. But that made me a little nervous." I'd never heard this imperturbable young man make such an admission before. "So what happened?" I asked, hoping to hear his description of Gary Matthews's prodigious home run. For a moment I thought he'd gone back to sleep because there was only silence at the other end of the phone.

"Didn't you hear?" he finally said. "The first guy up hit a home run."

"And how did that feel?" I asked still hoping to get some kind of reaction. "I heard his bat hit the ball," Liriano said. "But I couldn't see where it went. There are so many little circles on the ceiling of the Metrodome, it's hard to tell which is the ball."

I'd read some horror stories about the outdated, air-supported sports arena that has to be kept blown up like a huge balloon. Dave Kingman, I knew, had once hit a towering fly and was awarded a ground-rule double because the ball got stuck in one of the roof's drainage holes and never came down. Chili Davis likewise had hit what should have been a home run, but the ball caromed off a loudspeaker and was caught by the second baseman. Then there had also been rips in the ceiling that caused game delays. But I'd never heard anything about balls blending in with circles in the ceiling so they were hard to see.

"When will you get another chance to pitch?" I asked.

"They're keeping me in the bull pen," he said, still a little groggy, "so I don't know."

"Go on back to sleep," I urged. "I'll call you again in a couple of days."

That night a clubhouse eruption caused Matthews's home run to almost be forgotten, at least by everyone except Liriano. It all started when right-hander Kyle Lohse gave up five runs to the Rangers in the first two innings, forcing Gardenhire to yank him. Furious both with himself and the manager, Lohse went into the bat room behind the dugout and started throwing equipment around to blow off steam.

According to one source, as reported by La Velle E. Neal III of the *Minneapolis Star Tribune*, "When the right-hander stepped back in the dugout, Gardenhire said, 'That's going to be it, Lohse,'" implying that the pitcher would be traded. "'You're kidding me,' he replied. But the manager wasn't. 'We're in a pennant race and you gave up five runs in two innings.'" Later Lohse admitted stronger words than that might have been exchanged.

Still steaming, he went upstairs in the clubhouse and pounded some dents in the door to Gardenhire's office and the door to the next room, injuring a finger on his pitching hand during the tirade. But the bad feeling was more wide-spread than that. Some of the other pitchers were already simmering about the lack of run-support they received from the Twins' hitters—an average of 4.29 per game, the worst in the American League. And Lohse's was even lower than that.

General Manager Terry Ryan jumped into the breach and tried to cool things down, telling the players, "You win and lose as a ball club, not in separate factions."

Unfortunately for Liriano, it was in that turbulent atmo-sphere that he was staking his claim as a big leaguer. Those rumblings would have been more expectable down in the minors where the players are less experienced and more emotional. But if the Dominican was surprised to encounter such behavior in the majors, he didn't say. "The players have all been nice to me," is all he told me on the phone. "They call me Frankie."

On September 10 in an away game against Cleveland, the Dominican received his second chance, but only after reliever Travis Bowyer, who'd been called up from Roches-ter with him, took a turn on the mound and let the Indians break the game wide open. Bowyer had replaced J.C. Ro-mero with the bases loaded in the sixth inning. "When I got to the mound I was almost light-headed," the rookie reliever later confessed. "All I wanted to do is throw strikes." In-stead, he gave up a sacrifice fly, wild-pitched two more run-ners across the plate, and then allowed a run-scoring single. When he finally retired the side and came off the mound, he apologized to Romero for giving up his runs.

By the bottom of the eighth inning, when Liriano was called in from the bull pen, the Twins had scored only two runs on six hits and were behind 7-2. Perhaps he'd gained confidence from seeing how badly a fellow rookie could do. In any case, this time Liriano had full command of his pitches and struck out the side: Travis Hafner, Victor Martinez, and Ronnie Belliard, in that order.

In the ninth Justin Morneau pinch-hit a three-run homer to make the final score 7-5. The victory, however, gave the Indians a one-and-a-half game lead in the American League wild-card race, and put them seven-and-a-half games ahead of the Twins, whose situation had become almost hopeless. So Rick Anderson figured he could now risk giving Liriano a chance to start.

"It's amazing how far this kid has come since spring training," the pitching coach told me. "I couldn't believe how much better he was mechanically when he arrived here. Down in Fort Myers there were several things he wasn't doing right that kept him from executing his pitches. But between Stew Cliburn and Bobby Cuellar, they cleaned up his delivery."

Nevertheless, Rick had seen further room for improvement. In Liriano's first relief stint against Detroit, the pitching coach noticed he was overthrowing his fastball, apparently because he didn't trust it. "It was throw hard as he could, or just throw sliders because they won't be able to hit them," Rick claimed. "Then in the last game against Cleveland, I told him, 'Don't worry about getting swings all the time. Just think about locating your pitches, throwing with the intention they're going to hit them.' The trouble was he was trying to make every pitch perfect."

Rick then explained how he'd played games with Liriano during practice to work on his pitch location. "He seemed to like that," Rick claimed. "I'd say, 'OK, bet you a dollar you can't hit that spot down and away with your fastball.' If he missed he'd say, 'Give me double or nothing,' and that's the way it went. Obviously, nobody won, but it forced him to locate his pitches, and not throw so hard. It was just basically getting him to command his pitches better."

Even though Stew and Bobby had both worked hard on the Dominican's arm motion to eliminate the pain he'd suffered earlier in his career, Rick thought it could still be smoother. "I worked with him on the finish of his pitches, where his arm and body ended up."

Rick said he also urged him not to rely on his slider so much. " 'Just because you're getting swings on it is no reason to forget your fastball and changeup,' I told him. 'You've got three above-average major-league pitches. If at the end of the game, you've thrown 90 or more pitches and 40 of them are sliders, that's going to take a toll on your arm.'"

I asked Rick if he thought Liriano would be ready to join the rotation next year. "It all depends on how things break down," he replied. "Joe Mays is gone, so there's one spot. And I hear rumblings about Lohse. It isn't certain we're going to keep him." But one thing was clear, the pitching coach wasn't going to commit himself on Liriano's role next year, even though he expressed great admiration for him. "He's a very level-headed kid," Rick declared. "Very quiet in the clubhouse. Keeps to himself, so you can't ever tell if he's done bad or good."

Finally on September 14 Liriano was given his first start in an away game against Detroit. Ironically, it was because his idol Johan Santana injured a finger that he got the chance. In five scoreless innings he gave up only two hits and a walk, and struck out six. However, he had just struck out four Tiger batters in a row before a downpour in the third inning interrupted what promised to be a dazzling starting debut.

"If the rain had continued a little longer, I would have taken him out," the manager said. "I was worried that his arm might have gotten cold." Perhaps it did because Curt Granderson, the first batter he faced after the rain-delay, clubbed a two-run homer. After that Liriano retired seven batters in a row and erased the other two with an inning-ending double play.

Liriano wasn't charged with the loss because the Twins tied it up in the eighth inning before losing 4-2 in the ninth.

Rick Anderson was impressed. "We're really excited," he told Gordon Wittenmyer of the *St. Paul Pioneer Press*. "It's going to be fun having him around for more starts, and for 15 more years."

Ron Gardenhire was equally admiring. "He threw some great breaking balls and some great changeups," the manager said. "He had better location with those than with his fastball. But his fastball was jumping. I thought he handled himself well against some very good hitters." Even Art Trammell, the Detroit manager, lauded the young hurler's effort. "He throws in the mid-90s, with a slider and a good changeup. That's pretty impressive, especially for a left-hander."

Perhaps it was the cold during his second major-league start, a raw 61-degree night in Oakland's McAfee Coliseum, or perhaps Liriano just lost his concentration. In any case, the Athletics showed him what happens when you throw balls instead of strikes. After six runs, six hits, three walks, and a whopping 93 pitches in three-and-two-thirds innings, the young left-hander was gone, knocked out of the game by what Ron Gardenhire called "a bunch of big-time hitters."

"I learned something from this," is all Liriano said to the local reporters after the game. "You can't get behind in the count."

His difficulties that night started right in the first inning when he walked the lead off batter Mark Ellis, who then scored on Jason Kendall's double, giving Oakland a 1-0 lead. Liriano breezed through the second, but in the third with two outs, Kendall singled and scored again, this time on Mark Kotsay's double. But it was the fourth inning that finally did the Dominican in.

Once again he walked the lead off batter, Joe Payton, and the second batter, Scott Hatteberg, as well. Hiram Bocachica followed with a scratch infield single, loading the bases with no outs. That brought up Nick Swisher, the A's hard-hitting rookie-of-the-year candidate.

If only briefly, Liriano then showed why the Twins were so high on him. He struck out Swisher with a fastball that caught the outside corner of the plate and fanned Marco Scutaro swinging. With two outs, but with the bases still loaded, it looked like he might escape from the inning unscored on, provided he could also get the hot-hitting Mark Ellis out. That tense situation brought Rick Anderson out to the mound for a brief confab with his young leftie.

Whatever the pitching coach said must have bolstered Liriano's confidence because he blew a fastball past Ellis for strike one. Next it was catcher Joe Mauer's turn to visit the mound. Liriano followed his instructions, throwing a changeup for another strike. The next pitch, a ball, brought Mauer back out to the mound for yet another chat. Again, Liriano threw a changeup, apparently not trusting his fastball. Ellis saw it coming and hit a soft liner to right field, scoring Payton and Hatteberg.

Ron Gardenhire decided Liriano had learned enough lessons for one night and replaced him with Matt Guerrier, who was greeted with a two-run single giving Oakland a 6-1 lead. Oakland went on to win 8-3, Liriano being charged with his first major-league defeat.

"I threw that pitch to Ellis the way I wanted," he was quoted by the *Pioneer Press* as saying, suggesting that Mauer might have requested a fastball. "But that's the way it is," he added.

Actually, Rick Anderson wasn't so unhappy with Liriano's performance. "He showed some poise in situations that often rattle young pitchers," he declared. "He didn't throw a bad pitch to Ellis. It was a low-and-away changeup." But then he added, "I could see he was overthrowing again. Things he got away with down in Double-A and Triple-A, he can't get away with here."

When I talked to Liriano on the phone the next day, I could tell he was subdued. I wondered if he was following Rick Anderson around like a puppy, the way he kept at the heels of Bobby Cuellar after a poor showing in Rochester. "It was cold, but my arm felt good," was all he said before ending our conversation.

Things didn't go much better for the Dominican during his third start. But this time he was facing the White Sox in Chicago, who six weeks later would be crowned the World Series Champions. He became rattled in the third inning when Aaron Rowand hit a run-scoring triple, followed by a tremendous two-run homer by Paul Konerko. In six innings Liriano gave up four runs on five hits and three walks. But he also struck out eight of Chicago's vaulted hitters, who it turned out couldn't be contained in the World Series by the likes of Roger Clemens and Andy Pettitte.

Back home in the Metrodome on September 30, Liriano received his last chance to prove that he was ready to join the Twins' rotation. It was his fourth start, and second against the Tigers. He was determined not to fumble this opportunity. "My arm feels very good," he told me on the phone a day earlier. And it must have, because in seven innings he allowed only two runs on five hits, leaving the game with the Twins ahead 3-2 for his first major-league victory. (The final score was 7-3.) For the second game in a row, he struck out eight. It was also discovered after the game, he'd amassed 237 strikeouts during the season, more than any other pitcher in professional baseball. But perhaps even more impressive was the fact that he didn't walk one Detroit batter.

"In his first three starts, he was all over the place with his fastball," Rick Anderson said after the game. "Tonight he looks like he belongs." Ron Gardenhire echoed the same thought. "He's going to have an opportunity to make this ball club in spring training," the manager declared. "He impressed the heck out of the staff."

The next day I phoned Justin Olson to find out if he was aware of Liriano's first major-league victory. Since the two of them had started the season together with the Rock Cats, I was eager to hear his reaction. "Sure," he said. "I saw the box score on majorleaguebaseball.com." I could tell from his voice that he was enjoying Liriano's success vicariously, just as I was. "Wasn't that great!" he exclaimed.

Olson, it occurred to me, was taking inspiration from his former teammate's rapid rise to the majors. Perhaps it was giving him more hope about his own career. After all, he was bigger and stronger than the Dominican, and his fastball was only a mite slower. What he needed to do was to work on his slider and changeup. And I know he planned to do that next season. But in the meantime, he was back painting houses with his former boss. "I'm giving my arm a rest," he said. "But I'm working out every day to get in shape for spring training." I could tell he was eager to start throwing again.

A few weeks later, I was chatting with Jim Rantz, who had plotted Liriano's future with the Twins ever since he was acquired from the Giants. He, too, was excited about Liriano's first big-league victory. "Right now he's in the mix to be one of our starters next spring," he exclaimed proudly. "Joe Mays left. It was either renew his contract for 10 million or declare him a free agent, and that was a no-brainer." I wondered if they'd ever have to make that choice with Liriano. If so, it might not be such a no-brainer.

Rantz, however, was too modest to claim credit for the Dominican's success. "I give credit to those pitching coaches that worked with him," he said. "But obviously Liriano had the talent. And he didn't let anybody down."

That was true. It didn't matter whether he was throwing bullets for the Rock Cats, the Red Wings, or the Twins. Liriano gave his best every time he took the mound.

EPILOGUE

Most people, I suppose, would prefer a vacation at the seashore, in the mountains, biking, golfing, or even doing something more daring like rock climbing or white-water rafting. But for me nothing could have been more inspiring than a summer spent among all those minor-league players, their managers, coaches, and fans. Right from the beginning of my six-month odyssey, starting with spring training and ending with the play-off chases in two different leagues, I felt that I was seeing not just the game called "America's Pastime," but a slice of young America, glowing with energy and enthusiasm.

Traveling north, and at the same time through the farm-team hierarchy of the Minnesota Twins, it occurred to me that the promotion ladder for the players moving from the bottom to the top of their craft resembled the old guild system of the Renaissance: the apprentices starting down on a Rookie-League team or in Single-A; the journeymen moving up to Double-A, which is where Olson and Liriano began the season; and then as they become more skilled, being boosted again to Triple-A, before finally achieving the exalted status as masters, ready for the major leagues. Determination, persistence, and dedication are the best words I can think of to describe what propels them upward. As highly motivated competitors, they are imbued with all of those virtues.

Minor-league baseball I also discovered is very much of an equal-opportunity business that allows blacks, whites, Latinos, or men of any other race, color, or nationality to shine. At least as long as they keep on striving for excellence—or better yet, perfection—as they rise from rung to rung. That means honing their bodies and minds to give peak performances. Not just once a week as football players are asked to do, but for 144 days, 1,296 innings, and 3,888 outs, all in one season, with only a scattering of days off in between.

Are the demands so stringent, with so many different skills to learn, in any other business? Is the competition that tough in another field? Are the risks of failing greater in a different endeavor? I don't think so. That's why it was so exciting seeing those young athletes in action day after day, or more often night after night.

Every baseball contest has its unique situations, its moments of tension, despair, elation, and thrills. There are no long stretches of boredom, at least not for those who appreciate the complexities of the game. And there are no dull surroundings. Not in stadiums filled with exuberant fans that love baseball and know there'll be clowns and mascots accompanying the games, but no sleazy X-rated entertainment requiring parental supervision.

What's more, the young players themselves rarely fail to put on a good show, and they also love doing it. Is there another calling where pupils and their instructors more enjoy working together? Or a job that's more rewarding—not in terms of money earned during the learning years, but simply in satisfaction? Listen to the high-pitched clubhouse chatter and you'll realize that those involved don't think there's anything minor about the joys of being minor-leaguers.

And for me, the observer, the note-taker, the recorder of their words and actions, it couldn't have been more of a lark or a more interesting and informative experience. Just watching these young aspirants, these chasers of the dream, gain confidence as they scaled the steep climb to the majors was full of vicarious thrills for me.

It was hard saying good-bye to my newly acquired friends at summer's end. Not just to Liriano and to Olson, but to all of the others, too, as they disbanded and went into winter hibernation. I know that next spring when they emerge from their dugouts to take the field once again, I'll pore over the big-league box scores to see who made it and who didn't. Yes, and for many seasons to come, I'll keep on looking to see how they're doing. If they're doing well you can be sure I'll share their pride. Not because I had anything to do with their success or failure. Just because I was there.

ACKNOWLEDGMENTS

Many people deserve thanks for helping with this book. First and foremost the New Britain Rock Cats because it was my interest in that team for some years that eventually triggered the idea of covering two competing fastball pitchers, one a right-hander, the other a left-hander, both throwing from the same mound, as they chased the dream of becoming big leaguers.

Bill Dowling, President and General Manager of the Rock Cats, helped me get started and provided plenty of assistance along the way. His brother Bob Dowling, Director of Media Relations, provided considerable background information, while his assistant Courtney Nogas did many favors. Ken Lipshez, sports reporter for the *New Britain Herald*, was most generous in sharing his encyclopedic knowledge of the Rock Cats' players and the team's history. Manager Stan Cliburn and his twin brother and pitching coach Stew Cliburn always made themselves accessible. Jeff Dooley, the team's Director of Broadcasting, was ever ready to answer questions and provided essential statistical information.

ACKNOWLEDGMENTS

Dan Mason, General Manager of the Rochester Red Wings, couldn't have been more cooperative. Chuck Hinkel, Director of Media Relations, provided considerable help, as did Jim Mandelaro, sports reporter for the Rochester *Democrat and Chronicle*. The Red Wings' pitching coach Bobby Cuellar and Acting Manager Rich Miller willingly sat for long interviews.

Andy Gee, Director of Public and Community Relations for the Syracuse SkyChiefs, was very helpful, while Ron Gersbacher, Team Historian, provided essential background information.

Bill Wanless, Vice President of Public Relations for the Pawtucket Red Sox, made me feel most welcome. PawSox Manager Ron Johnson and pitching coach Mike Griffin gave me their expert opinions.

Lukas McKnight, a scout for the Chicago Cubs, provided insights about pitching that were extremely valuable to this non-expert.

The Minnesota Twins organization could not have been more cooperative right from spring training in Fort Myers, Florida, to the end of the season in Minneapolis. Jim Rantz, Director of Minor Leagues, was particularly helpful, granting frequent interviews. Rick Knapp, Coordinator of Minor League Pitchers, provided valuable information, as did Assistant General Manager Wayne Krivsky. Pitching Coach Rick Anderson showed great patience in answering my questions. Mike Herman, Manager of Media and Player Relations, handled my many requests most graciously.

I also feel indebted to editor Matt Harper, formerly of M. Evans and Company, who first grasped and appreciated the idea of this book. Rick Rinehart, who acquired the book for Taylor Trade Publishing after it took over M. Evans, was great to work with and very helpful, as was Production Editor Jehanne Schweitzer. As always, I want to thank Carol Mann my literary agent, who played an important role in the book's publication.

My friend Nat Carnes conducted an important interview for me in Spanish. Several other friends provided warm hospitality along my travel route: Dick Miller, President of Hartwick College, Ralph and Eleanor Graves, Don and Shareen Swinton, Stacey Smith, Arnold VanDenburgh, Betsy Phelps, and Carol Detweiler.

My wife Helen, not an ardent fan, nevertheless gave up a good part of her spring and summer to watching baseball games without a whimper. I am most grateful for her patience and support.

INDEX

INDEX

191